THE COMPLETE IDIOT'S GUIDE® TO

Foreign Currency Trading

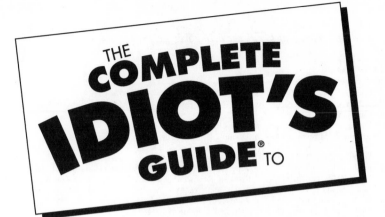

THE COMPLETE IDIOT'S GUIDE® TO

Foreign Currency Trading

*by Gary Tilkin
and Lita Epstein*

ALPHA

A member of Penguin Group (USA) Inc.

To all my friends at GFT, the best Forex dealing company in the world!

ALPHA BOOKS

Published by the Penguin Group

Penguin Group (USA) Inc., 375 Hudson Street, New York, New York 10014, U.S.A.

Penguin Group (Canada), 10 Alcorn Avenue, Toronto, Ontario, Canada M4V 3B2 (a division of Pearson Penguin Canada Inc.)

Penguin Books Ltd, 80 Strand, London WC2R 0RL, England

Penguin Ireland, 25 St Stephen's Green, Dublin 2, Ireland (a division of Penguin Books Ltd)

Penguin Group (Australia), 250 Camberwell Road, Camberwell, Victoria 3124, Australia (a division of Pearson Australia Group Pty Ltd)

Penguin Books India Pvt Ltd, 11 Community Centre, Panchsheel Park, New Delhi—110 017, India

Penguin Group (NZ), cnr Airborne and Rosedale Roads, Albany, Auckland 1310, New Zealand (a division of Pearson New Zealand Ltd)

Penguin Books (South Africa) (Pty) Ltd, 24 Sturdee Avenue, Rosebank, Johannesburg 2196, South Africa

Penguin Books Ltd, Registered Offices: 80 Strand, London WC2R 0RL, England

Copyright © 2007 by Gary Tilkin and Lita Epstein

International Standard Book Number: 978-1-59257-588-6
Library of Congress Catalog Card Number: 2006934448

09 08 07   8 7 6 5 4 3 2 1

Interpretation of the printing code: The rightmost number of the first series of numbers is the year of the book's printing; the rightmost number of the second series of numbers is the number of the book's printing. For example, a printing code of 07-1 shows that the first printing occurred in 2007.

Printed in the United States of America

Note: This publication contains the opinions and ideas of its authors. It is intended to provide helpful and informative material on the subject matter covered. It is sold with the understanding that the authors and publisher are not engaged in rendering professional services in the book. If the reader requires personal assistance or advice, a competent professional should be consulted.

The authors and publisher specifically disclaim any responsibility for any liability, loss, or risk, personal or otherwise, which is incurred as a consequence, directly or indirectly, of the use and application of any of the contents of this book.

Most Alpha books are available at special quantity discounts for bulk purchases for sales promotions, premiums, fund-raising, or educational use. Special books, or book excerpts, can also be created to fit specific needs.

For details, write: Special Markets, Alpha Books, 375 Hudson Street, New York, NY 10014.

Publisher: *Marie Butler-Knight*
Editorial Director: *Mike Sanders*
Managing Editor: *Billy Fields*
Senior Acquiring Editor: *Paul Dinas*
Development Editor: *Nancy D. Lewis*
Production Editor: *Kayla Dugger*

Copy Editors: *Keith Cline and Jennifer Connolly*
Book Designer: *Trina Wurst*
Cover Designer: *Rebecca Harmon*
Indexer: *Julie Bess*
Layout: *Chad Dressler*
Proofreader: *John Etchison*

Contents at a Glance

Contents

Introduction

Foreign currency trading gives you the opportunity to participate in the world's largest and most liquid market, known as Forex. More than $1.9 trillion U.S. dollars exchange hands daily.

The Forex market moves rapidly, with currency prices changing by the second. No single event, individual, or institution can rule this market. It's truly uncontrollable by any single entity because of its large liquidity.

Some traders see very large profits from trading in this market, but always remember that the market is highly speculative and volatile. While you can make a lot of money on a trade, you can also lose a lot on a trade.

Take the time to learn how to research your potential trades using both the fundamental and technical analysis tools we introduce to you in this book. Develop your own strategies for trading and test those strategies using demonstration accounts before you start trading your own money.

Remember, though, you should never trade Forex unless you're using money you can afford to lose. **Forex is a high-risk endeavor.**

How We've Organized the Book

You'll start exploring the world of foreign currency trading by learning how Forex got started and how it operates today. Then you'll explore how currencies differ from country to country. Next, we explore the trading basics. Then we'll introduce to the tools for trading.

We've organized this book into four parts:

Part 1, "Exploring the World of Money," looks at why you should consider trading Forex, then delves into how the Forex market got started and introduces you to the language of money. You'll also find resources for how to follow the money in daily news reports.

Part 2, "Deciphering Money Differences," gives you the opportunity to learn why currency values change and how the foreign exchange markets work. Then we'll take a closer look at the safest currencies to trade—currencies of the developed world. We'll also explore the more exotic currencies—emerging nations whose currencies may be worth considering once you understand the foreign currency market, its risks, and how to trade in it.

Part 3, "Trading Basics," introduces you to what computer hardware and software you'll need to trade, then introduces you to the basics of technical and fundamental analysis to help you research your potential trades. Then we explore the various risks you must take in order to trade in the Forex market.

Part 4, "Tools for Trading," explores how you can develop your own money strategies, as well as the basics for actually placing your trades. In addition, you'll find information about Forex mini accounts. We also alert you to ways to avoid getting caught up in Forex fraud.

Extras

We've developed a few helpers you'll find in little boxes throughout the book:

def•i•ni•tion

These will help you learn the language of Forex trading.

 ### Capital Cautions

These will give you warnings about things you need to avoid.

Currency Corn

These will explore interesting facts and other details about Forex trading.

 ### Wealth Builders

These will give you ideas for how to set up your own Forex trading business. You'll also find help with tips about resources you can use.

Acknowledgments

We'd like to give a special thanks to Kelly Quintanilla, whose attention to detail and assistance with all the content in this book helped make this a friendly user's guide for our readers. We'd also like to thank our editors at Alpha Books for all their help in making this book the best it can be: Paul Dinas, acquisitions editor; Nancy Lewis, development editor; and Keith Cline and Jennifer Connolly, copy editors.

Disclaimer

Foreign exchange trading involves high risks, with the potential for substantial losses, and is not suitable for all persons. The high degree of leverage can work against you as well as for you. The possibility exists that you could sustain a loss of some or all of your initial investment and therefore you should not invest money that you cannot afford to lose. Trading programs or strategies discussed in this book are for educational purposes only and are based on hypothetical or simulated performance results, which have certain inherent limitations. Because these trades have not actually been executed, the results may not have accurately compensated for the impact, if any, of certain market factors, such as lack of liquidity. Hypothetical or simulated trading programs are designed with the benefit of hindsight to illustrate strategic trading concepts, but no representation is being made that any account will or is likely to achieve profits or losses similar to the results being shown. Any opinions, news, research, analyses, prices, trading strategies, or other information contained on websites or publications mentioned in this book are provided as general market commentary, and do not constitute investment advice. Before deciding to trade foreign exchange you should carefully consider your investment objectives, level of experience and risk appetite. You should be aware of all the risks associated with foreign exchange trading, and seek advice from an independent financial advisor if you have any doubts.

Trademarks

All terms mentioned in this book that are known to be or are suspected of being trademarks or service marks have been appropriately capitalized. Alpha Books and Penguin Group (USA) Inc. cannot attest to the accuracy of this information. Use of a term in this book should not be regarded as affecting the validity of any trademark or service mark.

Part 1

Exploring the World of Money

Why trade foreign currency? Who trades it? In this part, you learn the answers to these questions and many more. You'll also learn how foreign exchange trading got its start.

The world of foreign exchange trading includes spots (and we're not talking about the type you find on dogs), forwards, options, and futures (and not the reading-the-tea-leaves type). We end this part by telling you how to locate news about the money markets and give you information to decide whether foreign exchange trading is right for you.

Teen
Wolf?
Michael J. Fox

Chapter 1

Why Trade Foreign Currency?

In This Chapter

◆ Finding out about Forex

◆ Discovering Forex players

◆ Exploring market structure

If we lived in a world where there was only one currency, there would be no foreign exchange market or fluctuating rates; but that's not how our world works. Instead we have primarily national currencies, and the foreign exchange market is an essential mechanism for making payments across country borders.

The foreign exchange market creates a way to transfer funds between countries and to purchase things in other counties. In this chapter, we look at what the foreign exchange market is and who trades foreign currency.

What Is Forex?

Forex is actually a short way of saying foreign exchange currency trading. Today the Forex market is by far the largest and most liquid market in the world. On average more than US$1.9 trillion is traded each day in the foreign exchange market. That's several times more than the daily volume in the world's second-largest market—the U.S. government securities market. In fact, Forex trading volume translates to more than US$200 in foreign exchange market transactions every business day of the year for every man, woman, and child on Earth!

Not only is the total volume hard to fathom for most people, the sheer volume of some individual trades can involve much more money than most people deal with in their entire lifetimes. It's not uncommon to hear of individual trades in the US$200 million to US$500 million range.

It's a fast-moving market, too. Price quotes for a currency pair can change as often as 20 times a minute, or every 3 seconds. The most active exchange rates can change up to 18,000 times during a single day. Actual price movements tend to be in relatively small increments, which also makes this a smoothly functioning and liquid market.

Foreign currency is exchanged in financial centers around the world, but the largest amount of currency actually changes hands in the United Kingdom. Well, changing hands may not be a good metaphor, because most of the transactions are done by electronic transmission, and paper currency is not really moved from one trader to another. Instead, an initial trade of foreign currency with one dealer leads to a number of different transactions over several days as various financial institutions readjust their positions (the open trades held by a trader).

In fact, a foreign exchange dealer buying dollars in any institution around the world is actually buying a dollar-denominated deposit in a bank located in the United States or the claim of a bank outside the United States based on the dollar deposit located in the United States. That's true no matter what currency you trade. A dealer buying a Japanese yen, no matter where he makes the purchase, is actually buying a yen deposit in a bank in Japan or a claim on a yen deposit in a bank in Japan.

Currency Corn

Where do most foreign exchanges take place? About 32 percent of all currency trades are handled through financial institutions in the United Kingdom, even though the British pound is not as widely traded as some of the other key currencies, such as the U.S. dollar, the euro, the Japanese yen, and the Swiss franc. U.S. financial institutions rank second in the volume of foreign exchange transactions handled, but that's a distant second—just 18 percent of foreign exchange transactions are handled by U.S. institutions. Japanese financial institutions rank third, with 8 percent of the transactions passing through their doors. Singapore is a close fourth, with 7 percent.

The United Kingdom is the most active financial trading center because of London's strong position as the international financial center of the world, where a large number of financial headquarters are located. According to a foreign exchange turnover survey completed in the late 1990s, more than 200 foreign exchange dealer institutions in the United Kingdom reported trading activity to the Bank of England, whereas only 93 in the United States were reporting to the United States Federal Reserve Bank of New York.

London has a major advantage over U.S. markets because of its geographic location. Because it is in the center (in regard to its time zone), the normal business hours for London financial institutions coincide with other world financial centers. Its early-morning hours overlap with a number of Asian and Middle Eastern markets, and its afternoon hours overlap with the North American market.

The Forex market is a 24-hour market almost 6 days a week. The markets are closed for only a short period of time on the weekends. As some financial centers close, others open; so the foreign exchange market can be viewed in terms of following the sun around the earth.

The 24-hour market means that exchange rates and market conditions can change in response to developments that can take place at any time. This differs significantly from the stock or bond markets, which primarily trade only when the exchanges are open. Although there is some overnight trading of stocks, it's a limited market with a lot less liquidity or volume.

If you learn about major news that might impact a foreign currency in which you trade, you have 24-hour access to act on that news. But if you learn about something regarding a stock you hold after the closing bell, you probably won't find a way to trade it until the next business day. This greatly decreases the chances of market gaps in Forex trading that can be found with stock trading.

Although 24-hour access might sound like a great opportunity, it can also create a money-management nightmare. As a trader, you must realize that a sharp move in a foreign currency exchange rate can occur during any hour, at any place in the world. Large currency dealers use various techniques to monitor markets 24 hours a day, and many even keep their trading desks open on a 24-hour basis. Other financial institutions pass the torch from one geographic location to another rather than stay open around the clock.

The volume of currency traded does not flow evenly throughout the day. Over any 24-hour period, there are times of heavy activity and times when the activity is relatively light. Most trading takes place when the largest numbers of potential *counterparties* are available or accessible on a global basis.

def•i•ni•tion

Every foreign currency exchange involves a pair of currencies traded between two parties. In order to trade a currency pair, you need to have a **counterparty,** such as a dealer who is willing to trade with you. For example, if someone wants to trade U.S. dollars for euros, one party must be holding the euros and one party must be holding the dollars in order to trade.

Business is heaviest when both the U.S. markets and the major European markets are open. That is when it is morning in New York and afternoon in London. In the New York market, nearly two thirds of the day's trading activity takes place in the morning hours before the London markets close. Activity in the New York market slows in the mid to late afternoon after the European markets close and before the Asian markets of Tokyo, Hong Kong, and Singapore open.

Who Trades Foreign Currency?

Although everyone talks about how the world is becoming a "global village," the foreign exchange market comes closest to actually functioning as one. The various foreign exchange trading centers around the world are linked into a single, unified, cohesive worldwide market.

Although foreign exchange trading takes place among dealers and other financial professionals in financial centers around the world, it doesn't matter where the trade occurs. Each trade is still being bought or sold based on the same currencies or bank deposits denominated in the same currencies.

So who is doing all this buying and selling? Only a limited number of major dealer institutions participate actively in foreign exchange. They trade with each other most often, but also trade with other customers. Most of these major players are commercial banks and investment banks. They're located in financial centers around the world, but are closely linked by telephone, computers, and other electronic means.

The central bank for most of these major dealer institutions is the *Bank for International Settlements (BIS)*, which covers the foreign exchange activities for 2,000 dealer institutions around the world. The bulk of foreign exchange trades are actually handled by a much smaller group. BIS estimates that 100 to 200 market-making banks worldwide handle the bulk of all trades.

def•i•ni•tion

The **Bank for International Settlements (BIS),** an international organization based in Basel, Switzerland, serves as a bank for the world's central banks. It fosters international monetary and financial cooperation by promoting discussion and policy analysis among central banks and the international financial community. It also conducts economic and monetary research.

Many different types of institutions and individuals are involved in the foreign exchange trading world. These include commercial banks, governments, broker/dealers, corporations, investment-management firms, and speculators/individuals. The sections that follow discuss the various participants.

Commercial Banks

Commercial banks handle the vast amount of commercial foreign exchange trading through the interbank market. A large bank may trade billions of dollars daily. Some of this trading is undertaken on behalf of customers, but even more of it involves trading in the bank's own accounts. Most of this trading is done through efficient electronic systems.

Governments

Most governments around the world conduct their foreign exchange trading through their central banks. These central banks control the money supply, inflation, and/or interest rates for their respective countries. In most cases they also try to maintain target rates set for their currencies by the government decision makers. In the United States, the target exchange rates are set by the U.S. Treasury Department working with the Federal Reserve, which actually conducts all foreign currency exchange for the U.S. government.

Sometimes central banks act on behalf of the government to influence the value of the country's currency. For example, if the U.S. government believes the currency is weak, the Federal Reserve starts buying U.S. dollars and even encourages other friendly nations to do so to boost the value of the dollar. If the dollar is thought to be too strong, the Federal Reserve begins selling U.S. dollars on the foreign exchange market or encourages other countries to do so. Governments can also adapt new economic policies to affect the value of its country's currency.

Brokers or Dealers

Retail brokers or dealers act as intermediaries between the banks and individual traders. Individuals and companies who work through brokers or dealers do so because it gives them the ability to trade anonymously through an intermediary. Brokers or dealers also have much lower minimum trade size requirements than large banks, which allow individuals to access the market.

This retail foreign exchange market represents only about 2 percent of the total foreign exchange market. The volume of retail trades through dealers totals about $25 to $50 billion daily. All online trading of foreign exchange currency is done through retail dealers or brokers.

Most brokers do not provide individuals with direct access to the true interbank market because very few clearing banks are willing to process the relatively small orders placed by individuals.

Corporations

Corporations trade foreign currency primarily so that they can operate globally or invest internationally. For example, a U.S. manufacturer may buy parts from a manufacturer in Singapore. When it comes time to pay for those parts, the U.S. manufacturer will need to pay for them with Singapore dollars.

Investment-Management Firms

Investment-management firms, which manage large accounts for other entities, including pension funds and endowments, trade foreign currency for the portfolios they manage, which enables them to buy foreign securities, including stocks and bonds, for their clients' portfolios. In most cases, these transactions are secondary to the actual investment decision; in some cases, however, the investment-management firms do speculate for their clients with the goal of generating profits on the currencies traded while limiting risk. Most investment-management firms place their Forex transactions through a dealer.

Speculators

All individuals who participate in the foreign currency market are considered speculators. Although you may hear controversy about the role of speculators in the foreign exchange market, they do provide an important function for the market. They provide a means for companies or people who don't want to bear the risk of foreign exchange trading to find an individual or institution that does want to take on that risk for the reward of future profits.

The largest speculators in the world of foreign exchange currency are hedge funds. These funds trade for a group of wealthy individuals and institutions that want them to use aggressive strategies in the hopes of reaping large profits.

Hedge funds can use strategies not permitted by mutual funds, including swaps and derivatives. (Read Chapter 3 for a full explanation of these terms.) Hedge funds are restricted by law to no more than 100 investors per fund, so minimum investment levels are high, ranging from $250,000 to more than $1 million per investor. Hedge fund managers not only collect a management fee for their work, they also all get a percentage of the profits, usually around 20 or 30 percent.

Forex Market Structure

Every country has its own infrastructure for its currency, including how foreign market operations must be conducted. Each country enforces its own laws, banking regulations, accounting rules, and tax code and operates its own payment systems for settling currency trades.

The foreign exchange market is the closest market to one operating in a truly global fashion, with currencies traded on essentially the same terms simultaneously in many financial centers. But you must be aware that there are different national financial systems and infrastructures to execute transactions.

In Chapter 5, you learn how currencies change value. You can find out more about individual countries and their currencies in Chapters 6 and 7. You find out about trading platforms in Chapter 8. Then Chapters 9 and 10 introduce you to tools for analyzing trading opportunities. Chapter 11 discusses the risks you face as a currency trader. Then Chapters 12 through 15 discuss the tools for trading, including money strategies, how to place orders, and alternative ways to trade. Chapter 16, the last chapter, warns you about money fraud and tells you how to avoid it.

The Least You Need to Know

- The foreign exchange currency market (Forex) is the largest and most liquid market in the world.

- Most foreign currency is traded by major dealer institutions (such as commercial banks or governments), with individual traders making up only 2 percent of the US$1.9 trillion global market.

- If you want to participate in the foreign exchange market, you will be considered a speculator.

Chapter 2

How Forex Started

In This Chapter

- ◆ Back in Babylon
- ◆ Agreeing at Bretton Woods
- ◆ Smithsonian settlements
- ◆ Monetary system in Europe
- ◆ Forex today

The foreign exchange market as we know it today is relatively new. It was started just a little more than 30 years ago, in 1973. But, of course, money has been around a lot longer than that. In this chapter, we review how money got started and how the current foreign exchange market developed.

Starting in Babylon

You must travel all the way back to the ancient kingdom of Hammurabi (third century B.C.E.) in Babylon to find the origins of banking. In those days, the royal palaces and temples served as secure places for the safe-keeping of grains and other commodities. People who deposited their commodities in the palaces and temples were given receipts that they could use to claim their commodities at a later date or give to others in payment for something else. These bills became the first known form of money.

Egypt also started a similar system of banking, providing state warehouses for the centralization of harvests. The written orders that depositors received were used to pay debts to others, including tax gatherers, priests, and traders.

Prior to these systems of deposits and receipts, the barter of goods was the primary way a person paid for things. Egypt moved from these paper notes to introduce the first coins. The earliest countable metallic money was made of bronze or copper from China. Other objects used for coins were spades, hoes, and knives, also known as tool currencies. The ancient Greeks during the time of Julius Caesar used iron nails as coins.

When people engaged in foreign exchange, which was primarily in connection with military activities, the primary currencies used in trade were precious metals. Initially, precious metals were traded by weight, but a gradual transition was made from weight to quantity.

During the Middle Ages, the need for a currency other than coins or precious metals arose. Middle Eastern moneychangers were the first to use paper currency rather than coins for trade. These paper bills represented transferable third-party payments of funds. They gradually became more accepted in foreign currency exchange trading, which made life much easier for merchants and traders. Regional currencies began to flourish.

From the Middle Ages to World War I, the foreign exchange markets were relatively stable. Not much speculative activity occurred. After WWI, however, the world of money changed. The foreign exchange markets became volatile, and speculative activity increased tenfold. Speculation in the foreign exchange market was not looked on as favorable by most institutions or the general public. The Great Depression of 1929 slowed the speculative fever considerably.

The dominant world currency before WWII was the British pound. In fact, the British pound got the nickname "cable" because the U.S. dollar was originally compared against it, and the U.S. dollar and the

British pound were the first currencies traded by telegraphic cable. The British pound lost its seat at the top of the currency world during WWII because Germany launched a massive counterfeiting campaign to destroy the power of the pound. All confidence in the pound was lost during WWII.

The U.S. dollar, which was in disgrace since the market crash of 1929, emerged from WWII as the currency of choice, which is still true today. The U.S. dollar remains the favored currency for most foreign exchanges. The U.S. economy boomed after WWII, and the United States emerged as a world economic power. The other big advantage of the United States was that it was one of few countries that hadn't felt the ravages of war on its own shores, so its massive infrastructure was still intact.

Bretton Woods Accord

After the war, the world's economy was in shatters. Something needed to be done to design a new global economic order and put all the pieces of the global economy back together. The United Nations Monetary Fund convened a global monetary and financial conference in Bretton Woods, New Hampshire, with representatives from the United States, Great Britain, and France, as well as 730 delegates from all 44 allied nations, to design a new global economic order.

The allies decided to hold the conference in the United States because it was the only place in the world not destroyed by war that was suitable for the conference. The conference ended with an accord, aptly named the Bretton Woods Accord, which established a system of international monetary management with rules for commercial and financial relations among the world's major industrial nations. The delegates hammered out the accord during the first three weeks of July 1944.

As part of the system of rules and procedures to regulate the international monetary system, the Bretton Woods Accord also established two key institutions—the *International Bank for Reconstruction and Development (IBRD)* and the *International Monetary Fund (IMF)*, which became operational in 1946 after a sufficient number of countries ratified the agreement.

def•i•ni•tion

The **International Bank for Reconstruction and Development (IBRD)** initially served as a vehicle for the reconstruction of Europe and Japan after World War II. Today it fosters economic growth in developing countries in Africa, Asia, and Latin America, as well as the post-Socialist states of Eastern Europe and the former Soviet Union. The **International Monetary Fund (IMF)** oversees the global financial system. It monitors exchange rates and balance of payments for foreign exchange transactions, and provides technical and financial assistance when requested by individual member counties.

The U.S. dollar emerged from Bretton Woods as the world's benchmark currency. It became the currency against which all other nations would measure their own currencies as they struggled to rebuild their economies.

One of the chief features of the new Bretton Woods system of foreign exchange was an obligation for each country to adopt a monetary policy that pegged the value of their currency to the U.S. dollar. The price of the U.S. dollar was pegged to gold at $35 per ounce, which became known as the gold standard.

Each country had to maintain its currency within a fixed value—plus or minus 1 percent—in terms of its peg to the U.S. dollar. This is known as a *fixed exchange rate.* The IMF was given the ability to bridge temporary imbalances of payments. The central bank of each country was required to intervene in the foreign exchange market if its country's exchange rate fluctuated more than 1 percent in either direction. The agreement initially served to bring stability to other countries and the global foreign exchange market. It succeeded in reestablishing stability in Europe and Japan. Until the 1970s, the Bretton Woods system helped to control economic conflict and achieve the goals set by the leading countries involved, especially the United States.

def•i•ni•tion

A **fixed exchange rate** is a type of exchange rate regime in which a currency's value is matched to the value of an individual country's currency or a basket of other countries' currencies.

Initially this system worked well and helped to fuel the world's economic growth, but the system eventually fell under its own weight. As more and more countries converted their dollars to gold, the U.S. gold reserves dwindled. Pressures started to build on the gold peg, and an attempt to ease the problem started in 1968 when a new system called special drawing rights (SDR) was established. Dollar exchange between banks was done using SDRs and was managed by the International Monetary Fund. Countries were encouraged to hold dollars rather than convert those dollars to gold.

By 1971, the United States had enough gold to cover only about 22 percent of its reserve obligations. There was no way the United States could cover the paper dollars at the exchange rate of $35 per ounce of gold as set by the Bretton Woods Accord.

Currency Corn

Today the gold held by the United States is held at the U.S. Mint in Fort Knox, Kentucky. The gold depository opened in 1937, and the first gold was deposited there in January of that year. The highest gold holdings for the United States were in December 1941, when 649.6 million ounces were on deposit. Today, only 147.3 million ounces are left. Gold is held as an asset of the United States at a book value of $42.22 per ounce, or $6.2 billion total, but the market price of gold in June 2006 was $574 per ounce.

On August 15, 1971, President Nixon single-handedly closed the gold window and made the dollar inconvertible to gold directly, except on the open market—removing the U.S. need to balance the value of the dollar to the value of the gold held in its reserves. He made this decision without consulting with other members of the international monetary system and even without talking with the State Department.

Nixon's shocking move killed the Bretton Woods Accord and threw the entire world's monetary system into shock. After the shock wore off, the United States led the efforts to develop a new system of international monetary management. During the next several months, the United States held a series of multilateral and bilateral negotiations with other countries known as the Group of Ten to try to develop the new system. Participating countries were Belgium, Canada, France, Germany, Italy, the Netherlands, Sweden, Switzerland, the United Kingdom, and the United States. Today the Group of Ten still exists, but Japan has joined its ranks, bringing the total to 11 countries, although it is still called the Group of Ten.

Smithsonian Agreement

In December 1971, the Group of Ten met at the Smithsonian Institution in Washington, D.C., and created the Smithsonian Agreement, which devalued the dollar to $38 per ounce with trading allowed up to 2.25 percent above or below that value. Dollars could not be used to convert directly to gold. Instead, the Group of Ten officially adopted the SDR system, and the IMF held the responsibility of keeping the system in balance.

The United States continued its deficit spending, and the value of the U.S. dollar continued to fall. Gold's value began floating on the international markets, and its value gradually edged up to $44.20 per ounce in 1971 and $70.30 per ounce in 1972. Countries abandoned any peg to the U.S. dollar and let their currencies float. By 1976, all the developed countries' currencies were *floating*, and exchange rates were no longer the primary way governments administered monetary policy.

Today the currencies of developed countries float, but many of the emerging countries still peg the value of their currency to the U.S. dollar or to a basket of currencies from a number of countries. In Chapter 7, we discuss the key emerging countries, many of which use some type of fixed-rate regime.

def•i•ni•tion

A **floating** exchange rate is an exchange rate regime in which the value of a currency fluctuates according to the foreign exchange market, instead of being pegged to a specific commodity (such as gold) or a specific currency (such as under the Bretton Woods system where currencies were pegged to the U.S. dollar).

European Monetary System

At about the same time as the Smithsonian Agreement, European countries established a European Joint Float. The nations that joined this system included West Germany, France, Italy, the Netherlands, Belgium, and Luxembourg. The basic system was close to the exchange rate regime established at Bretton Woods.

The European Joint Float failed at about the same time as the Smithsonian Agreement, but the decision among the Europeans to work together economically remained in place. The European countries began working together officially in 1957, long before the European Joint Float, under a treaty that formed the European Economic Community.

When the European Joint Float failed, the European nations worked together to form the European Monetary System (EMS) in 1979, which included most of the nations of the European Union. The goal of the EMS was to stabilize foreign exchange and counter inflation among the members of the EMS.

Periodic adjustments raised the values of the currencies whose economies were strong and lowered the values of the weaker ones. By 1986, a simpler system based on national interest rates was used to manage the currency values.

By the early 1990s, the EMS started to show strains, especially after Germany was reunited. Many European countries had very different economic policies, and faced varied economic conditions. Great Britain permanently withdrew from the EMS in 1991.

The EMS began efforts in the 1990s to establish a common currency in Europe. Its first step was to create the European Central Bank in 1994. By 1998, the bank was responsible for setting a single monetary policy and interest rate for the nations that chose to participate.

At the same time as the European countries moved to coordinate currency exchange, they also worked toward political and defense cooperation. The European Union (EU) was formed in 1992 with the Treaty of Maastricht.

By 1998, the first members of the European Central Bank were Austria, Belgium, Finland, France, Germany, Ireland, Luxembourg, the Netherlands, Portugal, and Spain. All cut their interest rates to a nearly uniform low level with the hope that this would promote growth and prepare for the unified currency. In 1999, the unified currency, the euro, was adopted by these countries.

Euro coins and notes did not begin to circulate until January 2002. Within two months, local currencies were no longer accepted as legal tender within the countries that had adopted the euro.

Great Britain is not the only European nation that has decided not to adopt the euro. Denmark and Sweden also decided to maintain their currencies. Citizens of all three countries oppose the adoption of the euro.

None of the countries that joined the EU since the fall of the Soviet Union have adopted the euro either, but several are working to meet the economic requirements to do so. Countries must meet strict economic guidelines before becoming part of the EMS and adopting the euro. These requirements set limits on allowable government deficits and interest rates.

Today's Foreign Exchange Markets

Today's system of floating exchange rates is not a carefully planned system. Instead, it was one born by default as the Smithsonian Agreement and the European Joint Float failed to gain momentum. Yet the foreign exchange market is by far the largest and most liquid market in the world today.

The floating system allows the values of currencies to rise and fall based on the basic laws of supply and demand. When the supply of a particular currency is high, the price (relative exchange rate) of the currency begins to drop because there is more supply available than demand. The opposite is true when the supply of a currency is tight. When less money is available for trade, the price (relative exchange rate) of the currency goes up because more people want the currency than what is available for purchase. You learn more about the principles of supply and demand in Chapter 5.

Major currencies today move independently from other currencies. They can now be traded by anyone from individual retail investors to large central banks. Central banks do intervene occasionally to influence the exchange rate for their country's currency.

What are the key developments that made the foreign exchange market so vibrant and liquid? These developments include the following:

◆ The flexibility countries have today to choose either a floating exchange rate or a fixed exchange rate.

◆ Financial deregulation moves throughout the world that included elimination of government controls and restrictions on foreign exchange in nearly all countries. This permits greater freedom for national and international financial transactions, and greatly increases global competition among financial institutions.

◆ Internationalization of savings and investments provides fund managers and institutions around the globe with large sums available for investing and diversifying across country borders to maximize returns.

◆ Broader trends toward international trade liberalization within a framework of multilateral trade agreements encourage the globalization of business.

◆ Major technological advances have led to rapid and reliable execution of financial transactions, to reduced costs, and to instantaneous real-time transmission of vast amounts of market information worldwide.

The Least You Need to Know

◆ There are two types of currency exchange regimes—fixed rate and floating. The developed countries all use a floating exchange rate. Many emerging countries use a fixed exchange rate, most often pegged to the U.S. dollar or a basket of currencies.

◆ Although the Bretton Woods Accord and its fixed exchange rate regime helped to rebuild the world economy after WWII, it ultimately failed.

◆ The euro, the unified currency of Europe, was first adopted in 1999 and is rapidly becoming a key currency in the Forex marketplace.   2/21/09   10 years old

◆ Today the foreign exchange market is by far the largest and most liquid financial market in the world.

Chapter **3**

Understanding Money Jargon

In This Chapter

- ◆ Reading the spots
- ◆ Going forward
- ◆ Finding swaps
- ◆ Checking out options
- ◆ Looking for futures

Trading in the world of money means you must learn an entirely new jargon to understand what the traders are talking about. You'll hear traders talk about spot and forward transactions, swaps, options, and futures. This chapter introduces you to these terms and explains how you use them to trade foreign currency.

Spot Transactions

A spot transaction is the simplest type of transaction in the world of foreign exchange. It is simply the exchange of one currency for another. The spot rate is the current market price, also known as the benchmark price.

The actual transaction does not require immediate settlement or payment "on the spot." The settlement of a spot transaction happens within two business days after the trade is made, which is also known as the "trade day." The trade day is the day the two traders agree to the terms of the spot transaction.

This two-day period gives the traders time to confirm the agreement and arrange for the clearing of the funds through a financial institution, such as an international bank. Remember, many times these transactions are taking place between traders in two different countries and two different time zones, so it does take time for the clearing of funds.

The only spot transaction in the United States with a settlement period of one day is the U.S. dollar to Canadian dollar exchange.

Pricing Spot Transactions

Every currency being traded has two prices: a buying price and a selling price. The selling price is the price at which the sellers want to sell, and the buying price is the price at which the buyers want to buy. These are also known as the bid and offer prices, where the bid is the price at which a *market maker* will buy a specified currency pair, and the offer is the price at which the market maker will sell the pair. The market maker provides a quote with the bid and ask prices for customers. The difference between these two prices is called the spread.

def•i•ni•tion

In the foreign exchange world, a **market maker** is a bank or Forex dealer that provides publicly quoted prices for specific currency pairs. Market makers add liquidity and provide a two-sided market. International banks serve as market makers for more than 70 percent of the foreign exchange market. Retail, or individual, customers typically go through licensed Forex dealing firms that act as market makers because these firms can access the prices and liquidity of the international banks while providing individuals with market access.

Quoting Spot Exchange Rates

Spot exchange rates can be quoted in two ways: as a "direct" quotation or as an "indirect" quotation. A direct quote is one in which the amount of the domestic currency (i.e., dollars and cents if you are in the United States) is given per unit of the foreign currency. An indirect quotation is quoted in the amount of the foreign currency per unit of domestic currency. For example, in the United States, a direct quote for the euro would be 1.25 USD = 1 EUR. An indirect quote would be 0.80 EUR = 1 USD.

You may also hear the phrase "American terms." The phrase is used in the United States and refers to a direct quotation for U.S. dollars per one unit of the foreign currency. In Europe, you might hear the phrase "European terms," referring to a direct quotation for someone in Europe from their currency per one unit of U.S. dollar. If you're in the United States and hear the phrase "European terms," that means you are being given the quote from the perspective of the foreign currency per one U.S. dollar.

In 1978, in an attempt to integrate the foreign exchange market into a single global market, the U.S. market changed its practices to conform to the European market. So today most quotes are given in European terms, as the foreign currency per one U.S. dollar.

Another set of terms you will likely hear when talking about foreign currency trading on the spot market is "base" and "terms" currency. The base currency is the underlying or fixed currency. For example, in European terms, the U.S. dollar is the base currency because it is the currency in the transaction that is fixed to one unit. The terms currency in the transaction is the foreign currency being quoted as a pair to the U.S. dollar. When you hear a quote, the base currency is stated first.

When a market maker quotes a currency for a trade in the spot market, he quotes it at the price at which he will buy or sell the currency per one unit of the base currency. For example, suppose you request a quote on a USD/CHF spot transaction. (USD is the ISO code for the United States dollar, and CHF is the ISO code for the Swiss franc.) The spot transaction may also be called the "dollar-swissie." The market maker could respond with a quote of 1.4975/85, which means that the market maker is willing to buy CHF at a price of 1.4975 per one U.S. dollar and sell CHF at a price of 1.4985 per one U.S. dollar.

When you get a quote on a currency pair, it is most often presented to the fourth decimal place. This is called a "pip." A pip is the smallest amount that a currency pair can move in price. This is similar to a "tick" on the stock market.

If a dollar is not part of the transaction, the exchange is done at what is called "cross-rate trading." The base currency is always the currency listed first in the trade, and the pricing currency is listed second.

Forward Transactions

If you don't want to settle a transaction within two business days, you can also trade using an outright forward transaction. In this transaction, you trade one currency for another on a pre-agreed date at some time in the future, but it must be three or more days after the deal date. The forward transaction is a straightforward single purchase or sale of one currency for another.

The exchange rate for a forward transaction usually differs from the rate for a spot transaction because the buyer and seller making the deal know the rates will fluctuate in the future and try to make their best estimate of what the future rate will be. When the forward transaction is executed, the buy and sell price is fixed, but often no money changes hands. Sometimes foreign currency dealers ask customers to provide collateral in advance.

Who Uses Forward Transactions

Companies use outright forward transactions for many different purposes, including future expenditures, hedging, speculating, and investing. One of the most common uses is to plan for a future expenditure.

For example, a U.S. company that knows it will need to pay for parts from a factory in Japan will execute an outright forward transaction to be able to plan for the exact cost of the parts based on the forward transaction price. That way, even if the foreign exchange price changes dramatically, the company can still depend on the agreed price for the parts.

Outright forwards in major currencies are available from dealers for standard contract periods, also known as "straight dates." These periods can be 1, 2, 3, 6, or 12 months into the future. You can make arrangements for "odd-date" or "broken-date" for contract periods in between the standard dates, but these types of trades can be much more expensive.

Setting Rates for Forward Transactions

When setting the rate for a forward, two factors impact the price: the spot rate of the currency and the interest rate differential between the currencies. In setting the price, the market maker neutralizes the impact of the interest rate difference between the two currencies named in the forward transaction.

Although spot transactions are quoted in absolute terms, say x francs per dollar, forward transactions are quoted in differentials, which are premiums or discounts from the spot rate based on the interest rate differential. The differential is calculated in basis points to neutralize the difference in interest rates. For example, if interest rates are higher for the Swiss franc than the U.S. dollar, the number of basis points calculated is subtracted from the base spot price for the Swiss franc to offset the differential.

Foreign exchange traders know that for any currency pair, if the base currency earns a higher interest rate than the terms currency, the base currency will trade at a forward discount. If the base currency earns a lower interest rate, the base currency will trade at a forward premium, at or above the spot rate.

Swaps

If you don't want to buy another currency, but just want to borrow it for a certain period of time, you can use a foreign exchange swap (FX swap). An FX swap allows you to exchange one currency for another and then re-exchange back to the currency you first held.

Banks and others in the dealer market use FX swaps to shift temporarily into or out of one currency for a second currency without having to incur the risk of a change in the exchange rate, which could happen if they were to hold an open position.

The use of FX swaps is similar to borrowing and lending currencies on a collateral basis. FX swaps provide traders with a way to use the foreign exchange markets as a funding instrument. They are used by traders and other FX market participants in managing liquidity, shifting delivery dates, hedging speculation, and taking interest rate positions.

There are two legs to an FX swap that settle on two different value dates, but it is counted as one transaction. The two parties involved in the swap agree to exchange the two currencies at a particular rate on one date (the "near date") and to reverse the payments, usually at a different rate, on a specific date in the future (the "far date"). If both dates are less than one month from the deal date, it is called a "short-dated" swap. If one or both dates are one month or more from the deal date, it is known as a "forward swap."

Although an FX swap can be attached to any pair of value dates, in reality a limited number of standard maturities (length between the near date and far date) account for most swap transactions. The first leg (near date) of the FX swap usually occurs on the spot value date, and for about two thirds of all FX swaps the second leg (far date) occurs within a week. Longer FX swaps are available for one month, three months, or six months. Many foreign dealers arrange odd or broken dates for their traders, but the costs for those are higher than the standard maturities.

Buying or Selling?

FX swaps can be either a buy/sell swap, which means that you buy the base currency on the near date and sell it on the far date, or a sell/buy swap, which means you sell the base currency on the near date and buy it on the far date. For example, if you buy a fixed amount of pound sterling spot for dollars (exchange) and sell those pounds sterling six months forward for dollars (re-exchange), that is called a buy/sell sterling swap.

Pricing FX Swaps

The cost of the FX swap is set by the interest rate differential between the two currencies being swapped. The amount of interest that could be earned during the period of the swap is used by the dealer to calculate the price of the swap.

In calculating the cost for the swap, the dealer uses the spot rate and adjusts it for the interest rate differential between the base currency and the terms currency for the number of days of the swap. This calculates the borrowing and lending rates for the currencies involved. The rates are then used in a second calculation to determine the swap points that will be added or subtracted to determine the price.

Currency and Interest Rate Swaps

In addition to FX swaps, there are also interest rate swaps, which involve an exchange of a stream of interest payments without an exchange of principal; and currency swaps, which include an exchange and re-exchange of currency plus a stream of fixed or floating interest payments.

The currency swap gives companies a way to shift a loan from one currency to another or shift the underlying currency for an asset. A company can borrow funds in a currency different from the currency needed for its operations. The currency swap provides protection from exchange rate changes related to the loan.

Companies sometimes use currency swaps to gain access to a particular capital market otherwise unavailable to them because of currency restrictions in that particular market. They can also be used to avoid foreign exchange controls or taxes.

Currency swaps are not as popular as interest rate swaps because interest rate swaps do not involve the exchange of principal, so the cash requirements and the amount of risk are lower. When you enter into an interest rate swap, the two parties involved in the swap agree to make periodic payments to each other for the period of time set in the swap. The principal amount on which the interest is based is called the "notional amount of principal," but the amount of principal does not change hands.

The most common form of interest rate swap is one in which the payments are calculated by setting a fixed rate of interest to the notional principal amount, which is then exchanged for a stream of payments calculated by using a floating rate of interest. This is called a fixed-for-floating interest rate swap. If both sides of the cash flows are to be exchanged using a calculation based on floating interest rates, it's called a money market swap.

Interest rate swaps are used by commercial banks, investment banks, insurance companies, mortgage companies, investors, trust companies, and government agencies for many different reasons, the most popular of which are as follows:

♦ To obtain lower-cost funding

♦ To hedge interest rate exposure

♦ To buy higher-yielding investment assets

♦ To obtain types of investment assets that might not otherwise be available

♦ To implement asset or liability management strategies

♦ To speculate on the future movement of interest rates

Foreign Currency Options

You don't have to actually buy any currency to speculate in the foreign currency market. You can buy a foreign exchange or currency option contract. This contract gives you the right but not the obligation to buy or sell a specified amount of one currency for another at a specified price on (or in some cases, depending on the contract, before) a specified date.

Options don't have to be exercised (meaning to actually buy or sell the currency). The holder can decide not to exercise his or her option. If the holder decides not to exercise the option on the specified date, the option expires. The holder doesn't have to come up with any funds on the specified date, but does lose any money spent to buy the option.

There are two types of options. A call option is the right, but not the obligation, to buy the underlying currency on a specified date. A put option is the right, but not the obligation, to sell the underlying currency on a specified date.

The person who purchases the option is the holder or buyer. The person who creates the option is the seller or writer. The price of the option is set by the seller and includes a premium that the buyer pays the seller in exchange for the right to buy or sell the underlying currency at some future date. The price at which the option is bought is called the "strike price" or "exercise price."

The buyer of the option only risks losing the amount of money he or she paid in premium to buy the option. The writer of the option's risk is unbounded because he or she must come up with the underlying currency if the option's buyer decides to exercise his or her right on the specified date in the contract—even if the cost of buying or selling that underlying currency is considerably higher than when the option was originally written.

Options have been around for a long time, but only started to flourish in the foreign exchange market in the 1980s. Their popularity was aided by an international environment of floating exchange rates, deregulation, and financial innovation. Currency options started on the U.S. commodity exchanges, but are available in the over-the-counter market, too. Options are very popular, yet they make up a very small share of foreign exchange trading.

Wealth Builders

If you want to trade in options, your best place to start is through one of the U.S. exchanges. In the United States, options on foreign currencies are traded on the Philadelphia Stock Exchange (www.phlx.com) and the Chicago Mercantile Exchange (www.cme.com). You can also trade options on the U.S. dollar index and on the euro index at the New York Board of Trade (www.nybot.com). In the near future, Forex dealers such as GFT will offer Forex options.

Exchange-Traded Currency Futures

Another way you can get involved in the foreign currency exchange market without actually exchanging foreign currency is through exchange-traded currency futures. These are contracts between two parties to buy or sell a particular non-U.S. dollar currency at a particular price on a particular future date.

When you actually enter into the contract, no one is buying or selling any currency; it's just a contract with a promise to purchase a foreign currency at some future date. In reality, most futures contracts are canceled before maturity, and only about 2 percent result in delivery. Futures contracts are primarily used as a tool to hedge other financial positions or to speculate in the foreign exchange market.

You may think that futures seem to be the same as outright forwards, but they are not. Futures are traded on organized centralized exchanges that are regulated in the United States by the *Commodity Futures Trading Commission*. Forward contracts are traded over the counter and are largely self-regulated, so they can be a much more risky transaction.

def•i•ni•tion

The **Commodity Futures Trading Commission** (www. cftc.gov) is a U.S. government entity that protects market users and the public from fraud, manipulation, and abusive practices related to the sale of commodity and financial futures and options. The commission's mission also includes fostering open, competitive, and financially sound futures and options markets.

The fact that futures contracts are channeled through a clearinghouse with the guarantee of performance on both sides of the contract makes them a much safer bet than forward contracts. It's much easier to liquidate a futures contract, too, because there is an established futures market. Also the high degree of standardization for the futures contracts means that traders only need to discuss contracts one wants to buy and the price for the contract. Transactions can be arranged quickly and efficiently.

Forward contracts do provide more flexibility in setting delivery dates. They tend to be for higher amounts, sometimes for millions of dollars. Futures contracts are much smaller and are usually set at about $100,000 or less. A trader who wants to buy more than that buys the number of contracts needed to hedge or speculate in the dollar amount desired. You can trade futures on the same exchanges mentioned in the "Foreign Currency Options" section of this chapter.

The Least You Need to Know

◆ Most developed-country currencies are sold at floating exchange rates on the spot market.

◆ You can arrange to buy foreign currencies at some future date using a forward transaction.

◆ You can swap foreign currency or an interest stream from foreign currency using one of three types of swaps: Forex swaps, currency swaps, or interest rate swaps.

◆ You can get involved in the foreign exchange market without actually buying and selling foreign currency by using options and futures contracts.

Chapter 4

Finding Information About Forex

In This Chapter

◆ Getting up-to-date news

◆ Finding forecast data

◆ Comparing Forex to other financial instruments

When trading Forex, you need to know a lot more than just the exchange rate between the two currencies you want to trade. You also need to know about the economic and political conditions of the countries whose currencies you plan to trade.

In addition, you want to watch for any dramatic moves in the value of either currency in the currency pair you plan to trade that might impact the value of that trade. You should also be aware of any upcoming economic announcements that could affect the volatility or the relative value of the currency you are considering trading, so that you can determine the best times to trade.

You might wonder whether currency trading is the best market for you to trade, or if some other market would be better for you, such as stocks or futures. This chapter examines the best places to get news about the currencies you are trading and compares Forex to other trading opportunities.

Getting the News About Money

When it comes to finding news about the financial markets, you may already be aware of the three top news sources:

◆ *The Wall Street Journal* (www.wsj.com) is the most respected daily business newspaper. You do need to buy a subscription to read the articles online, but you can get one for as low as $99 per year. The expense is well worth it, no matter what type of trading you plan to do.

◆ Bloomberg (www.bloomberg.com) is the leading global provider of financial news. It does have a radio and a television station, which is great if your local cable provider includes it in your package; but if not, you can always access its information online.

◆ *The Financial Times* (www.ft.com), which is based in London, provides an excellent overview of the financial news from a European perspective. When trading foreign currency, it's critical to understand the news from a global perspective.

In addition to these key financial newspapers, one excellent website that focuses entirely on Forex news is FX Street (www.fxstreet.com). There you can find breaking news about various currencies as well as upcoming economic events and economic indicators.

Author Gary Tilkin's company, Global Forex Trading, provides resources on its website to help you trade. The website includes commentary and forecasts from some of the leading experts in the Forex market and an economic calendar. You can find the information on his resources page at www.gftforex.com/resources. The site also provides real-time prices for currency exchange rates.

You should also read the key newspapers for whichever country's currency you plan to trade. Many times it will take days and sometimes weeks to learn about key news stories that impact only one country. If that country happens to be one in which you are trading its currency, you want to know the breaking news as soon as possible. The best way to do that is to read the national newspapers for the countries whose currencies you trade.

Staying Alert to Breaking Currency News

Coverage of breaking news regarding currency and other financial issues is best found on one of the top two financial cable networks:

♦ Bloomberg Television is a 24-hour news channel that reports on key financial news. The station has 750 reporters and editors in 79 bureaus around the world that focus on money and the markets.

♦ CNBC is a world leader for covering business news stories and broadcasts financial news highlights throughout the day. You can find more in-depth coverage of contemporary business issues during its evening programs.

FX Street, which we mentioned previously, also provides news alerts about currency in the "Latest Forex News" box on its home page.

Getting Forecasts on Major Currency

To make money trading foreign currency, it's helpful to read the forecasts about what is likely to happen to the value of the currency in the future. You can visit a number of excellent websites that give you forecasts from key foreign exchange analysts:

♦ Cornelius Luca, a respected foreign exchange analyst, writes a daily and weekly column that is posted on co-author Gary Tilkin's website at www.gftforex.com/resources/commentary.asp.

♦ FX World Trade (www.fxworldtrade.com) focuses on commentary and data for five key currencies and how the currencies are trading with the U.S. dollar, specifically the Japanese yen, Canadian dollar, euro, Swiss franc, and the British pound. It also provides forecasts regarding key economic news that could impact the value of the currencies.

♦ FX Street provides forecasts on key currencies from numerous analysts at www.fxstreet.com/nou/grups_continguts/ senseframesboa2.as. You can find forecasts and commentary about the U.S. dollar, the euro, the British pound, the Japanese yen, the Australian dollar, the Canadian dollar, the Swiss franc, and the Chinese renminbi.

Comparing Forex

You are probably asking, "Is trading Forex worth the risk?" and "How does it compare to other trading opportunities, such as futures and stocks?" or "Should I stick to a less-risky investment alternative?" The sections that follow discuss all these thoughts.

Forex vs. Futures

Forex gives the trader many advantages over trading futures. The biggest advantage Forex has is that you can trade the market 24 hours a day, and trading only briefly closes on the weekends. It is rare for you to face a period of illiquidity (not being able to trade) in the Forex market, whereas you are limited to the times the exchanges are open in the futures market.

If you hear news that could affect your positions at almost any time of day or night, you can trade on the Forex market, but you'll have to wait until the exchanges open on the futures market. This gives the Forex trader more flexibility and continuous market access, which just isn't available to the futures trader.

Forex traders have the advantage of three main economic zones that are linked throughout the world to give them trading opportunities throughout the day and night. For example, when the Pacific Rim markets, which include Japan and Singapore, begin to slow, the European markets of England, Switzerland, and Germany are just getting started. When the European markets are in full swing, the North American market opens, which includes the United States, Canada, and Mexico. When the United States markets begin to slow down in the evening, the Pacific Rim markets are just reopening.

Foreign exchange is the principal market of the world. The monetary volume (US$1.9 trillion a day) and participation in the Forex market far exceeds any other financial market, including futures or stocks. Because the market is so large and available 24 hours a day, it is not affected by trading programs that can easily manipulate the stock or futures market.

The Forex market offers some of the smoothest trends available in any market. Its 24-hour daily trading opportunity makes it a haven for traders who don't want to worry about gaps (differences between when the futures market closes and reopens) or price movements, erratic spikes, and other choppy market conditions that can be seen in the futures market. However, slippage can occur when a dealer's office is closed, during times of extreme market volatility, or during major fundamental announcements. Slippage is when orders are filled at a price worse than the stop price requested by the trader.

If you study any market trading throughout the civilized world, you can quickly see that money is the root of all pricing. Global finance is distributed and redistributed using money through many different channels and different financial *derivatives*.

Trading spot currencies can be done with many different methods, and you will find many different types of traders. You will find fundamental traders who speculate using mid- to long-term positions based on worldwide cash-flow analysis and fixed-income formulas, as well as economic indicators. We talk more about fundamental analysis in Chapter 10. You will also find technical traders who watch for patterns and indicators in consolidating markets. We talk more about technical analysis in Chapter 9.

def•i•ni•tion

Derivatives are a type of financial instrument that's value is dependent upon another instrument, such as a commodity, bond, stock, or currency. Futures and options are two types of financial derivatives.

Forex is where the "big boys" trade—that's all the major banking institutions in the world—but Forex can also provide the small speculator with the opportunity for large profit potential, although the trader also has to be prepared for the corresponding large risk of trading foreign currency.

Another big advantage for Forex traders is that the fees are typically less than those found in the futures market. All traders, whether in futures or Forex, will find that financial instruments have a spread, which is the difference between the bid (the price at which a buyer will buy) and ask (the price at which a seller will sell) price. In the Forex market, you only have to worry about the spread; in the futures market, however, you often have to pay commission charges, as well as clearing and exchange fees, on top of the spread.

Many currency dealers don't charge any additional fees to their customers for trading Forex. Instead, they make their money through revenues as a currency dealer, including proceeds from buying, converting, and holding currencies. They also earn interest on deposited funds and rollover fees. So as a currency trader, you will be able to find commission-free trading at the best trading prices.

A good currency dealer should be able to offer you a way to make quick decisions on your Forex trades without having to worry about how fees will impact your profit or loss. You also should not have to worry about any slippage between the price you see on your screen and the price at which your order will be filled. However, Forex dealers cannot guarantee that slippage won't occur when a dealer's office is closed, during times of extreme market volatility, or during major fundamental announcements.

Better leverage is another advantage you can find when trading foreign currencies rather than futures. Trading using leverage is also called trading on *margin*. Spot currency traders have one low-margin requirement for trades conducted 24 hours a day. Futures traders can have one margin requirement for "day" trades and a different margin requirement for "overnight" positions. This can decrease the overall tradability of the currency futures markets.

Margin rates in spot currency trading vary from .25 to 5 percent, depending on the size of the transaction. You can find currency dealers who give their customers one rate all the time, with no hassles and no *margin calls*.

def•i•ni•tion

Margin is the amount of money deposited by a customer that is required to be deposited to the broker or dealer. Margin is a percentage of the Forex or futures position value. A **margin call** is a broker's or dealer's demand on a customer to deposit additional funds into his or her account. Margin calls are made to bring a customer's account up to a minimum level.

Forex vs. Stocks

When trading Forex, you can primarily focus your attention on four major currency pairs (euro/U.S. dollar, U.S. dollar/yen, British pound/U.S. Dollar, and U.S. dollar/Swiss franc), with the potential to make a decent profit. These currency pairs are the most commonly traded, and the most liquid. You can add about 34 second-tier currencies for variation, but only if you commit yourself to the extra research time. With the majors, you can spend a lot less time on your computer researching potential trades and more time on other things you enjoy doing.

When you consider stocks, you have to choose among 8,000 stocks: 4,500 on the New York Stock Exchange and 3,500 on the NASDAQ. How do you pick the stocks you want to trade, and how do you make the time to continually research the companies you do pick?

Stocks are viewed by many as an investment vehicle, but in the past 10 years stocks have taken on a much more speculative role. Securities face more and more volatility every day, especially with the forces of day trading and other factors you can't predict.

How many times have you heard that a large mutual fund was buying a particular stock or basket of stocks and those trades created unexpected movement in a stock you held? Mutual funds can also influence the market at the end of the fiscal year, just to make the numbers look better on a financial report.

No matter what some firms may claim, the stock market can be moved by large fund buying and selling, and the movement can take place before you have time to react. It is not uncommon for a mutual fund to sell or buy a particular stock for a few days in a row.

You won't find these types of problems in spot currency trading. The liquidity of the market makes the likelihood of any one fund or bank controlling a particular currency very slim. Banks, hedge funds, governmental agencies, retail currency conversion houses, and individuals are just some of the participants in the spot currency markets, which are the most liquid markets in the world.

Another big advantage spot currency trading offers to traders is that there is no middleman, so it costs less to trade. If you work directly with a dealer, who is a primary market-maker, you do not deal through a middleman. However, brokers operate through a bank or an FCM, so they may charge additional fees to cover the added costs.

In the stock market, you have centralized exchanges, which means you have middlemen who run those exchanges, and they need to be paid, too. The cost of these middlemen can be in both time to do the trade and money. Spot currency trading doesn't have any middlemen. Traders can interact directly with the market maker for a particular currency who is responsible for pricing the currency pair. Forex traders get quicker access and cheaper costs than stock trading.

Analysts and brokerage firms are less likely to influence the Forex market than the stock market. Too many scandals have been exposed since 2000 that show how analysts told clients to buy a stock while calling it garbage (and worse) in e-mails behind the scenes. These analyst cheerleaders kept the Internet and technology moving upward, whereas stock investors unknowingly bought into companies that ultimately proved to be worthless.

Currency Corn

Wall Street's big brokerage houses paid $1.4 billion in fines to settle charges from regulators that they tricked investors into buying stocks during the boom years of the 1990s. The brokerage houses did not admit guilt, but they did agree to cut ties between their analysts and investment banking activities, which shared research. Two star analysts, Jack Grubman (telecom stocks) and Henry Blodget (Internet stocks) were banned from the securities business for life. Civil cases related to these charges are still winding their way through the courts.

The difference in trading foreign currency is that the primary market for the currency is driven by the world's largest banks and foreign governments. Analysts don't drive the flow of deals in the foreign currency market. All they can do is analyze the flow that is occurring.

If you trade in the stock market, you've probably found that there are different costs depending upon how you trade. You pay more fees if you call in your order or ask for specific types of orders, such as a stop or limit order to minimize your risk. You should not find additional costs when placing an order for trading in foreign currency.

Margins and leverage opportunities are much better in the Forex market, too. In spot trading, you can use your profits on open positions to add to those positions. That's something you might wish you could do when you own a hot stock and want to capitalize on the profits you've made by buying more of that stock. Although it's not possible in stock trading, you can do it when trading spot currency.

Forex vs. Other Less-Risky Investments

If you are concerned about the risks of Forex trading and prefer less-risky investments, such as bonds and mutual funds, Forex trading is probably not for you. If avoidance of risk is your primary investment concern, you probably won't be comfortable trading in the spot currency market.

Whether you are trading Forex, stock, or futures, you must be willing to take on risk and must understand that the money you use for trading could be lost. There is no insurance to protect your money (except occasionally offered on stock accounts), and you should only trade with money that you can afford to lose.

The Least You Need to Know

- ◆ Reading key financial newspapers daily is important for whatever type of trading you plan to do.

- ◆ Read the analyst forecasts regarding the currencies you trade or plan to trade. Foreign currency analysts cannot move markets the way stock market analysts can; instead, they provide an excellent overview of the key factors that do influence the price of the currencies they follow.

- ◆ Foreign exchange trading is not for you if you want to avoid risk entirely, but it can be a better trading opportunity if you want to assume risk in order to improve your profit potential. Foreign currency trading offers you 24-hour-a-day access to the most liquid market in the world.

Part 2

Deciphering Money Differences

Lots of things impact the value of currency. Economics, political developments, changing interest rates, stock news, inflation expectations, investment patterns, and government policies can all impact the value of money. We talk about *how* in this part. Then we introduce you to the key developing country and emerging country currencies you might want to consider trading.

Chapter

Why Currency Changes Value

In This Chapter

- ◆ Money and basic economics
- ◆ How politics impact currency
- ◆ Currency and interest rates
- ◆ Inflation and its money pressures
- ◆ International investors can move money values

Money makes the world go 'round, and lots of things can impact the value of that money. You can't control any of these factors that change the value of money, but you definitely need to understand what they are so that you can make tactical decisions about when to buy or sell a particular currency.

This chapter reviews the key factors that can impact the value of currencies, including basic economics, political change, interest rate changes, international investment patterns, inflation predictions, and money or tax policies adopted by governments and central banks.

Economics and Business Cycles

Currency, just like any other item that is bought or sold, can be impacted by the basics of economics and the business cycle. The *laws of supply and demand* are just as valid when talking about the value of currency as they are when talking about the value of any commodity.

When the supply of a particular currency is high, the price for that currency goes down as holders of the currency try to find ways to get rid of it. For example, if everyone decides that they don't want to hold U.S. dollars anymore and tries to sell them, to do so they would likely have to lower their price to find a buyer. In this case, there is more supply than demand.

You can compare this to the sale of real estate in your neighborhood. When there are a lot of houses on the market, they may sit unsold for many months. If someone must move because of a job change or some other reason, that person will likely price his or her home to sell (price it below what all other homes are listed for) to get it sold more quickly.

Conversely, when the supply of the currency is low and there are more people who want to buy it than there is currency available, the price of the currency goes up as buyers compete for the currency. In this case, there is more demand than there is supply. Using the same comparison, you can relate this to home sales in your neighborhood. When there are few homes available, buyers will offer the full asking price and sometimes bid that price even higher to be sure to get the home.

def•i•ni•tion

The **law of supply** states that as price rises, the quantity supplied rises; as price falls, the quantity supplied falls. The **law of demand** states that as price falls, the quantity demanded rises; as price rises, the quantity of demand falls. When supply and demand are in balance, that means at a certain price and quantity, the amount the buyer wants to buy is equal to what the seller wants to sell.

You may be wondering how a market could suddenly be flooded with a currency to increase supply and ultimately drive the price of the currency down. Well, that's one role governments and central banks take when they want to impact the value of a currency. I talk more about how the policies of governments and central banks impact the value of currency later in this chapter.

Governments can also decide they want the value of their currency to increase, and they have the buying power to buy currency and make the availability of their currency scarce. This will make the price of the currency rise.

Wealth Builders

As a currency trader, if you do see a rapid increase or decrease in the price of a currency you trade, be sure you understand why that movement is happening before jumping in yourself. One website that does an excellent job of covering the forces that impact currency values is FXstreet (www.fxstreet.com). London's *Financial Times* (http://news.ft.com/markets/currencies) also provides excellent coverage in its "Currencies" section.

Government manipulation is not the only thing that can impact the value of a currency economically. The action of businesses and consumers as a whole can drive currency values up and down. However, because the Forex market has so much volume, with more than US$1.9 trillion traded daily, it is highly unlikely that one single entity could impact the value of a currency for a significant period of time.

The good news for currency traders is that they have the potential to make money no matter what direction the market moves. Whether the business world is prospering and we're in the middle of a bull market (a market in which prices are rising and business is expanding) or we are experiencing a slowdown in the middle of a bear market (a market in which prices are dropping and business is contracting), it is still possible to make money during either condition by trading currencies.

The key is to know which kind of market each country is facing and how that market is impacting the value of the currency. Remember that each currency trade involves at least two countries: the country of the currency you are selling and the country of the currency you are buying.

Political Developments

Political changes can have the most dramatic effects on the value of a currency. They also can happen very quickly (such as a coup by the military). So when you choose the currencies you want to trade, be sure you understand the politics of the country for each currency you follow.

You may hear about some incredible opportunity for trading the currency of a developing country, but be very cautious with such rumors. The more unstable the country's politics, the greater the chance you will be burned in currency trading. Be very careful about trading on rumors, especially in developing markets.

Capital Cautions

As a beginning currency trader, stick to the major currencies, at least at first. Political changes can happen much more quickly and dramatically in the developing countries, which can significantly impact the value of that country's currency. Chapter 6 reviews the basics of trading in key currencies from developed countries and emerging countries.

Even in the most stable countries, after an election in which the party in power changes, the impact on the currency can be significant. For example, in the United States, if the current president and his party in power believe a strong dollar is good for the economy, the U.S. government can reduce the supply of its currency by buying up dollars and thus force the price to rise.

Conversely, if the party in power changes with the next election and the new president believes a weaker dollar will increase U.S. exports and decrease imports, the government could take moves to weaken the dollar (lower its price) by increasing its supply on the open market. So even in a very stable country, you may find that political change can impact the future value of a currency.

How the party in power manages the country's domestic economy can also be critical. When the economy is in a period of growth with relative price stability, the currency of that country will be in demand. Although if a country is facing political turmoil, high inflation, or has few marketable exports, its currency will be less attractive.

For example, policies of the Bush and Clinton administrations that created larger and larger imbalances, both in trade deficit and budget deficit, fueled the U.S. currency declines over the past few years against stronger currencies, such as the euro and yen. As the U.S. government pumps out trillions of dollars in new federal debt, financial markets will drive down the value of these bonds as these bonds create a future glut. Ultimately, the value of the dollar could suffer even more as investors move away from the dollar and U.S. government bonds to currencies and bonds they view as stronger or better investments.

Changes in Interest Rates

When interest rates go up or down, the value of a currency can fluctuate. When interest rates go up, the currency is more attractive to currency investors because they'll make more money holding it. So when interest rates rise, more traders and investors buy that currency, the supply of the currency becomes scarce, and the price of the currency rises.

The opposite happens when interest rates go down. Fewer investors want to hold on to the currency, especially if they can find a better deal someplace else. Many traders and investors start to sell the currency, and its supply goes up. As supply increases and demand decreases, the value of the currency goes down.

Be sure to watch the interest rate fluctuations in each of the countries whose currency you trade. Follow the pronouncements of the central banks and governments about their plans to raise or lower interest rates. Markets move rapidly on this type of news, and you can quickly get caught on the losing side if you hold a currency whose price is dropping because interest rates have just been lowered.

International Stock News

News about the stock market can also drive currency values up or down. Although the major stock markets (such as NASDAQ, New York Stock Exchange, American Stock Exchange, London Stock Exchange, and Tokyo Stock Exchange) get the most coverage, you'll find there are stock exchanges and stock news to be had in most developed countries and many developing countries.

When trading foreign currency, you need to keep your eye on the international stock market news, not only news from the U.S. exchanges. Keep an eye on stock index movements in any of the countries whose currency you trade. Stock market moves can impact the value of a currency.

Inflationary Expectations

Inflation and its impact on the economy can significantly impact the value of the currency, too, so you need to keep your eyes and ears open for news about any inflationary expectations within the countries you monitor.

Of course, one of the first things to be changed if the central bank or government believes inflation may be on the rise is the interest rates. Remember that interest rate fluctuations can have a major impact on the supply and demand for the currency and ultimately the price at which the currency will sell.

Currency of countries that are not raising their interest rates during an inflationary period will likely decrease in price, whereas the price of currency in countries that are increasing the interest rates will likely increase.

Inflation can also impact where imports and exports are bought and sold as prices rise or fall. This will change a country's *balance of payments* and ultimately impact the value of the country's currency.

def•i•ni•tion

The **balance of payments** measures the flow of money into and out of a particular country to other countries. Pieces of this calculation include a country's exports and imports of goods and services, as well as the transfer of financial capital. Basically, the balance of payments is the summary of all economic transactions between a country and all other countries during a particular period, usually a quarter (three months) or a year.

The payments and liabilities (debt) owed to foreign countries are listed as debits. The payments and obligations due from other countries are listed as credits. When that balance of payments is out of whack, especially if the country owes more than it receives, the value of the currency can drop.

Trade imbalance can lead to the loss of jobs, as we have seen in the United States, where 1.5 million U.S. jobs moved to China between 1989 and 2003. Servicing of debt can also increase as the country that owes more to other countries must make its debt issues (bonds) more attractive to buyers by raising interest rates.

The United States does have one huge advantage that enables it to run large trade deficits: the U.S. dollar is the primary currency for all oil trades with OPEC. Every country that wants to buy oil from an OPEC country must use U.S. dollars to buy oil. Some call these dollars petrodollars. That helps to prop up the value of the U.S. dollar.

Inflation occurs when too much money is available. The value of the money will decline and prices in the country will rise as exports become more expensive. When too little money is available, the economy will become sluggish, and unemployment will rise.

International Investment Patterns

Money (and currency buyers) flows to the currency where traders or investors can get the highest return with the least amount of risk. Investors flock to a country when stocks and bonds command a high rate of return with relatively low risk.

For buyers to buy those stocks and bonds, they first must buy the currency. That increases the demand for the currency, and the currency's price increases.

When you're trading foreign currency, don't only look at the charts of the currency moving up and down. You also want to follow news of what investors in other types of financial markets are doing.

You can get many clues by watching the flow of international investments. Read the key financial news sites, such as *The Wall Street Journal* (www.wsj.com), Bloomberg (www.bloomberg.com), *Business Week* (www.businessweek.com), and *CNN*

Wealth Builders

When you see investments in a country rise and the economy booming, you'll likely also see the value of that currency rise. If investors are taking flight and getting out of a country, selling off their holdings, the value of the currency will likely fall. Traders should watch investment patterns to find currency trading opportunities.

Money (http://money.cnn.com) to find information about investment waves to locate your next trading opportunity.

Policies Adopted by Governments and Central Banks

Governments and central banks can impact a currency's value using two key tools: foreign exchange rates and tax policy. Government officials closely monitor economic activity to keep the money supply at a level appropriate to achieve their economic goals. Money supply can be increased or decreased, which is usually done by changing the interest rate or manipulating the supply of money on the market.

In the United States, the government agency responsible for setting foreign exchange rates is the U.S. Treasury Department. The entity responsible for carrying out those decisions is the New York Federal Reserve Bank under the direction of the *Federal Open Market Committee* (*FOMC*) of the Federal Reserve.

def•i•ni•tion

The **Federal Open Market Committee (FOMC)** is a group of 19 people plus about 40 staffers. The 7 members of the Federal Reserve Board and 12 presidents of the Federal Reserve Banks make up the committee. When the committee takes a vote, only 12 of the people can vote: the 7 Federal Reserve Board members, the president of the New York Fed, and 4 of the other 11 Federal Reserve Bank presidents. Voting rights rotate among the bank presidents.

The U.S. Treasury can impact exchange rates. If the U.S. government believes the exchange rate does not reflect fundamental economic conditions, it can instruct the New York Fed to buy or sell currency in the foreign exchange market to impact the value of the U.S. dollar. Sometimes the United States works diplomatically with other countries to get them to intervene, too, by buying or selling U.S. dollars.

The New York Federal Reserve also acts as an agent on behalf of other countries' central banks and international organizations. When the New York Fed acts as an agent for another country or organization, these transactions do not necessarily reflect the policy of the U.S. government. These actions can be done openly through the Forex market, or they can be done discreetly through a confidential dealer in the brokers' market. I talk more about who the brokers are in Chapter 1.

Tax policy can also significantly affect the value of a country's currency. Tax policies can encourage or discourage investment by domestic businesses as well as by foreign investors.

How Traders Can Take Advantage of These Changes

Savvy traders learn to keep their eyes on all these factors as they look for opportunities to make money by trading currency. Key events to watch for include the following:

♦ News of political instability around the world drives up the value of currency from stable countries, such as the U.S. dollar, Japanese yen, Swiss franc, British pound, or the euro, as people seek safe havens in stable countries.

♦ A country's currency value can increase as foreign investors seek better interest rates in countries with more attractive interest rates than they can find in their own country. Watch interest rates move as you look for trading opportunities.

♦ The currency of a developing country that is making successful economic moves usually experiences an increase in that country's currency as foreign investors seek new investment opportunities. As you become a more experienced Forex trader, watch for an increase of investment dollars into a developing country; the currency may also increase in value.

Currency traders try to predict the behavior of other market participants. If they correctly anticipate the strategies of others, they can act first and beat the crowd. You basically have two possible currency strategies: buy currency at a low price hoping to sell it later at a higher price, or sell currency at a high price hoping to buy it back later at a lower price.

In trying to predict their best moves, currency traders who use fundamentals try to determine whether the current price of a currency reflects the true economic conditions in the country. They look at inflation, interest rates, and the relative strength of the economy to make a determination about the future value of the country's currency. If they believe the currency is undervalued, they buy it with the expectations that the currency's value will increase. If they believe the currency is overvalued and they own some of it, they dump it.

The Least You Need to Know

◆ Keep your eyes on the economic conditions in each of the countries whose currency you trade.

◆ When interest rates rise, purchases of that currency will likely increase, supply will become scarce, and the price of the currency will rise. The opposite happens when interest rates fall.

◆ Political change can greatly impact the value of a country's currency.

◆ Governments can impact the value of their currency through monetary and tax policy. They can intervene in the currency's value by changing the supply of the money on the market.

Chapter 6

Looking for Safety– Developed Country Currencies

In This Chapter

- ◆ Exploring developed countries
- ◆ Determining key economic factors
- ◆ Reviewing political factors
- ◆ Eyeing characteristics and trends

When you trade foreign currency, you should know the key economic and political forces that drive that currency's value. You also need to explore the characteristics and trends that will likely impact the future value of that currency.

This chapter reviews the key information you need to know about the generally lower-risk currencies from the developed countries—Australia, Canada, the European Union, Great Britain, Japan, New Zealand, Switzerland, and the United States.

We listed these countries alphabetically, not ranked by their popularity or by their potential for foreign currency trades.

Australia (Australian Dollar)

Although Australia is small compared to the other developed countries discussed in this chapter, its per capita *GDP* of US$32,000 compares in size to major Western European economies.

def•i•ni•tion

GDP or **gross domestic product** is the market value of all final goods and services produced within a country during a specified period of time. GDP is calculated as follows: GDP = consumption + investment + government spending + (exports − imports).

Services make up the lion's share of Australia's economy—70 percent. These components include finance, property, and business services. Major exports include coal, gold, aluminum, iron ore, and wheat; but Australia imports more than it exports. Its imports include machinery and transport equipment, computers and office machines, and telecommunication equipment and parts.

This extensive need for imports results in a large trade deficit for Australia, US$16.6 billion, driven primarily by a drought, weak foreign demand for many of its products, and strong import demand by its citizens. The country faces a national deficit of US$509.6 billion. Australia's biggest benefit is that it's the third-largest producer of gold.

In 2005, some economists feared that Australia's rapid increase in housing prices might drive the RBA (Reserve Bank of Australia) to increase interest rates to ease the speculative bubble and slow down the economy. The real estate prices appear to have peaked in 2005, which eased these worries.

Australia's economic policy maker is the RBA, which emphasizes economic reforms and low inflation in its management of monetary policy. The RBA meets 11 times per year on the first Tuesday of every month except January. The bank's board members discuss economic developments in the country and determine whether there will be any change in the interest rate, as well as other key economic decisions. Any changes in monetary policy are announced the next day.

Key characteristics and trends to watch if you are considering trading the Australian dollar (AUD) include the following:

◆ Australia is the third-largest producer of gold in the world. The AUD appreciates when gold prices increase and depreciates when gold prices decrease.

◆ Australia's export economy is primarily based on commodities, which can be sensitive to severe weather conditions that can affect its agriculture and related industries and negatively impact its GDP.

◆ Australia's high interest rate makes it a very popular currency to buy for carry trades. An example of a currency *carry trade* is to borrow $1,000 AUD from an Australian bank, exchange the funds into U.S. dollars, and buy a bond for an equivalent amount. As long as the bond pays more than the amount owed to the bank for borrowing the funds and the exchange rate does not move adversely, you can make a profit on this trade.

You can find a good summary about the political conditions and economy of countries by reading the Background Notes prepared by the U.S. State Department on its website at www.state.gov/r/pa/ei/bgn. Co-author Gary Tilkin provides up-to-date information about each of the developed countries' characteristics and trends on his company's website at www.gftforex.com/resources/currency/developed.asp. Another good source for country information is the *World Factbook* (www.odci.gov/cia/publications/factbook).

def•i•ni•tion

A **carry trade** is a foreign exchange strategy where a trader sells a certain currency with a relatively low interest rate and uses the funds to purchase a different currency yielding a higher interest rate. The trader attempts to benefit from the difference in the two rates.

Canada (Canadian Dollar)

Canada boasts the twelfth-largest economy in the world. It's also a major trading partner with the United States. In fact, more than 85 percent of its exports go to the United States, so the fate of its economy and dollar are very sensitive to the state of the U.S. economy.

Prior to the mid-twentieth century, Canada was primarily a rural economy, but since then it has grown into an industrial-based economy with the growth of manufacturing, mining, and service industries. Nearly 75 percent of its workforce is employed in a service-oriented occupation.

Canada manages its fiscal policy well and has a long-term budget surplus, which reduces its approximately US$600 billion national debt annually; but rising medical costs and their impact on the publicly funded health-care system does raise political and economic debates among its politicians.

Canada maintains a substantial trade surplus of US$47.1 billion with its main trading partner, the United States. Its major exports include motor vehicles and parts, industrial machinery, chemicals, plastics, wood pulp, timber, petroleum, and natural gas. With 178.9 billion barrels of proven oil reserves (which is the amount of recoverable petroleum from known reserves), Canada is second in the world behind Saudi Arabia.

The Bank of Canada sets Canadian monetary policy. It influences the economy primarily by ensuring price stability by adhering to an inflation target set by the Department of Finance. It achieves its inflationary targets by influencing short-term interest rates through its overnight lending rate to banks. Any changes in the interest rate are announced on eight scheduled dates during the year. You can find the schedule on its website at www.bankofcanada.ca/en/monetary/target.html.

The Bank of Canada periodically conducts foreign exchange market intervention by using the government's supply of foreign currencies in its exchange fund account. For example, if the Bank of Canada wants to offset a decline in the Canadian dollar (CAD), it buys CADs in foreign exchange markets with other countries' currencies, most often the U.S. dollar (USD). This creates a demand for CADs and helps support their strength or value. To be sure that this foreign exchange activity does not impact the local economy, the bank deposits the amount of dollars purchased into Canada's financial system. The bank does the exact opposite if it wants to weaken or lower the CAD on the foreign exchange market.

You can read about the bank's policies and strategies in a quarterly Monetary Policy Report and Update on its website on the same page as its interest rate schedule mentioned previously. Also published on that page weekly on Friday afternoons are key banking and money market statistics.

Wealth Builders

You can follow the Bank of Canada's interest rate and other economic policy decisions through updates on its website at www.bankofcanada.ca/ en/index.html. You can also find Canadian economic and fiscal information on the Department of Finance's website at www.fin.gc.ca/ access/ecfisce.html.

Key characteristics and trends to remember about Canadian currency include the following:

◆ The Canadian economy is highly dependent on commodities, so the CAD tends to increase when commodity prices increase and decrease when commodity prices decrease.

◆ Because Canada exports 85 percent of its products to the United States, its economy is highly sensitive to changes in the U.S. economy.

◆ Mergers and acquisitions between U.S. and Canadian companies occur regularly and can affect the value of both currencies.

◆ If Canada's interest rate is higher than the United States', the USD/CAD carry trade can become a popular way to make money.

European Union (Euro)

The European Union (EU) includes 25 member countries in Europe. Twelve of those countries have joined the European Monetary Union (EMU) and use the euro (EUR) as their currency. These include Belgium, Germany, Greece, Spain, France, Ireland, Italy, Luxembourg, the Netherlands, Austria, Portugal, and Finland. European Union members that have not yet adopted the euro include Cyprus, Denmark, the Czech Republic, Estonia, Hungary, Latvia, Lithuania, Malta, Poland, Slovakia, Slovenia, Sweden, and the United Kingdom.

In creating the EU, one of its primary goals was to adopt a common currency to strengthen the European countries' trade, as well as international political and economic positions. Income disparities and disagreements among the nations regarding certain EU policies have delayed adoption of the currency among all member nations, as well as the adoption of an EU constitution.

The EU's overall economy is the second largest—second only to the United States—with a GDP valued at US$12.18 trillion in 2005, which makes up 21 percent of the world's total gross product. The EU also has the third-largest workforce in the world, which is about a quarter of the size of China's labor force. Sixty-seven percent of the economy is based on service; but as one of the world's most technologically advanced industrial economies, its industries make up 27 percent of its GDP.

The EU is the largest exporter of goods and services, with US$1.318 trillion in annual exports from its member countries, including machinery, motor vehicles, aircraft, plastics, and pharmaceuticals. The United States imports 24 percent of the EU's products, which makes it the EU's most important trade partner. The formation of the EU and its significant clout on the world markets increases the bargaining power of its member nations.

The euro is gradually developing as a key reserve currency, and there has been a shift in the global money markets toward the euro and away from the U.S. dollar. The trend likely will increase the EU's leveraging power.

The European Central Bank maintains the purchasing power of the euro and seeks to maintain price stability within the member countries of the EMU. The six-member governing council of the bank meets twice monthly to discuss monetary policy. Monetary policy decisions are made during the first meeting of the month. The bank uses various open-market operations to influence interest rates and manage market liquidity, including monetary transactions, issuance of debt certificates, foreign exchange swaps, and long-term deposits.

Wealth Builders

You can follow the economic and monetary policy decisions of the European Central Bank at its website: www.ecb.int/home/html/index.en.html. Two key reports to watch are its Monthly Bulletin and its Statistics Pocket Book. The Statistics Pocket Book contains selected macroeconomic indicators for the individual member states of the EU, as well as comparisons between the EU, the United States, and Japan.

Key euro characteristics and trends to watch include the following:

◆ EUR/USD is usually the most liquid currency pair, which makes this a popular currency trade. The movements of this pair are used as the primary gauge of European and U.S. strength and weaknesses.

◆ Because the euro is the common currency for 12 countries, it's highly sensitive to the political/economic instabilities in any of its member countries.

◆ Follow the differential in rates between the U.S. 10-year bond and the 10-year German bond. This is a good indicator of euro movement.

Great Britain

Will it or won't it? If you ask that question about whether Great Britain will or won't join the EMU and give up its British pound (GBP), you can quickly send the money markets into a spin. Anytime the lead politicians in Britain mention that they favor adopting the euro, the British pound starts to drop in value. Politicians can just as quickly raise the value of the pound when they speak in opposition to the EMU and adopting its euro.

Why does Great Britain matter so much? It's the seventh-largest economy in the world, with a 2005 GDP of US$1.867 trillion. It's also the world's fifth-largest importer and seventh-largest exporter. The United States, Germany, and France are Britain's best trading partners. Britain's agricultural industry produces 60 percent of the country's food, a much more efficient industry than that seen in other European countries.

Britain also has significant coal, natural gas, and oil reserves. Its energy production makes up 10 percent of the country's GDP, one of the highest of any industrial nation.

Britain's workforce, however, is driven by service-oriented occupations, which employ 79.5 percent of its workforce. To strengthen its economic position and reduce its debt, the UK government greatly reduced public ownership and limited growth of social welfare programs. It has also raised taxes to support education, transportation, and health services.

The Bank of England (BOE) directs the UK's monetary policy. Its monetary policy committee sets interest rates to meet the inflation target set annually by the chancellor of the Exchequer. The Committee holds monthly meetings followed by announcements of state changes in monetary policy and interest rates. The BOE publishes two quarterly reports: the Inflation Report and the Quarterly Bulletin.

Wealth Builders

You can follow Bank of England announcements, as well as access its two key financial reports, the Inflation Report and the Quarterly Bulletin, on its website: www.bankofengland.co.uk.

The United Kingdom has outperformed most major economies with its economic policies, which makes it even more skittish about joining the EMU. The EMU has faced problems implementing the single monetary authority for the 12 countries under its umbrella.

The pound commands one of the highest interest rates for major industrialized country currencies. In fact, for the United Kingdom to join the EMU and adopt the euro, it would have to decrease its interest rate significantly. This interest rate decrease would encourage currency traders to sell the GBP and weaken the British pound.

Key characteristics and trends for the British pound that you should watch include the following:

- GBP/USD is one of the most liquid currency pairs in the world. Approximately 6 percent of all currency trading involves GBP.

- GBP provides holders with one of the highest interest rates among major markets.

♦ Watch interest rates between *UK gilts*/U.S. treasuries and UK gilts/German bonds for potential currency-movement indicators. These matches indicate the differentials in premium yield in fixed-income assets.

♦ Energy production makes up 10 percent of the UK's GDP. When energy prices increase, so does the value of the GBP.

def•i•ni•tion

The **UK gilt** is a government bond similar to U.S. Treasury bonds.

Japan

Japan boasts the world's fourth-largest economy and is the fifth-largest exporter in the world. It maintains an ongoing trade surplus, which was valued at US$99.4 billion in 2005. This surplus creates demand for the Japanese yen (JPY). The bad news that weighs down Japan's economy is that it also manages a fairly large national debt of US$1.545 trillion.

Japan's primary trade partners are the United States and China. Japan manages one of the world's largest and most technologically advanced industrial machines. Its industries produce motor vehicles, electronic equipment, machine tools, steel and nonferrous metals, ships, chemicals, textiles, and processed foods. Japan also owns more than half of the world's "working robots."

All is not good news for Japan. As a highly industrialized nation, it's heavily dependent on the import of raw materials and fuels. Its agricultural sector is small and highly subsidized.

Through the 1990s, Japan's economy suffered a major economic setback. Dramatic asset value drops, including a burst of the real estate bubble, left many of its developers and banks with bad debt and worthless collateral. Japan is still recovering from this economic downturn.

The Bank of Japan (BOJ), which directs the country's monetary policy, is working with the Japanese Ministry of Finance to fix the problems. The bank has poured funds into the ailing banks of Japan to prevent bankruptcies and attempt to grow the banks back to a healthier balance sheet. Therefore, the banking sector is very dependent on the government and its political whims. This makes the yen very sensitive to political developments, including pronouncements by government officials that indicate changes in monetary and fiscal policy.

The Bank of Japan seeks to maintain price stability as well as stability of the financial system. The BOJ's monetary policy board determines monetary policy at monthly policy meetings. The results of these meetings are announced in the Monthly Report of Recent Economic and Financial Developments. The bank also prepares a quarterly report called the Tankan Survey, an economic review of Japanese businesses.

Wealth Builders

You can access the Bank of Japan's key financial reports, the Monthly Report of Recent Economic and Financial Developments and the Quarterly Tankan Survey, at the BOJ's website: www.boj. or.jp/en.

Japan intervenes regularly to manage the value of its currency. The minister of finance instructs the BOJ when to buy or sell the yen to either raise or lower its value. The BOJ uses government funds to carry out the minister's orders.

Japan's currency frequently faces rapid appreciation because of its strong trade surplus. The minister asks for foreign exchange interventions when the yen (JPY) appreciates or depreciates rapidly in value, to maintain a steady USD/JPY rate, or to direct speculative current positions.

Key characteristics and trends for the Japanese yen that you should watch include the following:

◆ Economic and political problems in other Asian economies can have a dramatic impact on the Japanese economy and JPY movements.

◆ Trades involving the JPY can become very active toward the end of the Japanese fiscal year (March 31), as exporters move their dollar dominated assets.

◆ The JPY tends to be more volatile during the U.S. trading hours (7:20 A.M. to 2 P.M. EST) and during the Japanese lunch hour, which happens between 10 to 11 P.M. EST.

◆ Because the banking crisis is still a critical aspect of Japan's economic health, watch Japanese bank stock movements closely to find clues about JPY movements.

◆ The JPY has the lowest interest rate of all industrialized countries, so it is the primary currency sold in carry trades.

New Zealand

New Zealand manages a small economy compared to the other industrialized nations, with its 2005 GDP valued at just US$97.9 billion. Its population is equivalent to just half the population of New York City, yet the population inhabits more than 300 times the area.

New Zealand worked hard over the past 20 years to transform the country into an industrialized, free-market economy that competes globally. This work resulted in a boost to incomes, technological advances, and controlled inflation.

Trade of its agricultural products drives New Zealand's growth. Exports of goods and services make up 20 percent of the country's GDP. The country's trade deficit was US$2.36 billion in 2005. These factors make New Zealand's economic success heavily dependent on global performance. Its key trading partners include Australia, the United States, Japan, and China. Its national deficit is relatively small at US$57.67 billion.

New Zealand's agricultural base for its economy makes it highly sensitive to severe weather conditions that can damage its farming activities. Its economy can also be sensitive to weather conditions in Australia.

The Reserve Bank of New Zealand (RBNZ) manages the country's currency, the New Zealand dollar (NZD). Its monetary policy seeks to maintain stability and efficiency of the financial system, as well as meet the currency needs of the public. Working with the New Zealand minister of finance, the RBNZ outlines monetary policy in the Policy Targets Agreements (PTA). The most recent PTA requires RBNZ to keep inflation between 1 to 3 percent.

The bank does this by borrowing from or lending cash to New Zealand's financial institutions in open-market operations. In fact, New Zealand has one of the most open-market operations in the world. Each banking day at 9:30 A.M. in New Zealand, the bank announces details of its operations.

Wealth Builders

You can learn more about the Reserve Bank of New Zealand and its open-market operations at www.rbnz.govt.nz. You will find a link to its monetary policy on the opening page.

For the next 15 minutes, bidders submit bids with their interest rate demands. Based on these bids, the bank announces a minimum rate at which it will lend and a maximum rate at which it will borrow. If there aren't enough bids to fully offset the government's cash-flow needs, the bank then uses overnight operations to make up any shortages.

Key characteristics and trends you should watch in regard to the New Zealand dollar include the following:

♦ New Zealand's economy benefits from a strong Australian economy.

♦ Follow interest rate differentials between New Zealand and Australia, as well as interest rates yields of other industrial countries.

♦ The NZD is a commodity-linked currency, so as commodity prices increase, the NZD tends to appreciate.

♦ New Zealand's high interest rates tend to make the NZD a popular currency for carry trades.

Switzerland

Switzerland, known as a safe haven for money, is the place investors flock to when there is any uncertainty in the global marketplace. It gained its reputation as a safe haven because of the confidentiality its banks can offer depositors.

Switzerland boasts a low unemployment rate that is half that of the European Union. About 70 percent of its workforce is employed by banking and insurance firms catering to investors taking advantage of Switzerland's safe and confidential banking haven.

Germany is Switzerland's key trading partner. Other key partners include the United States, France, and Italy. The country maintains a trade surplus of US$13.6 billion, one of the highest in the world, and a national debt of US$856 billion. Its major exports include machinery, chemicals, consumer products, and agricultural products.

The Swiss National Bank (SNB) manages the Swiss franc (CHF) and Switzerland's monetary policy, which strives to maintain price stability.

The bank seeks to maintain no more than a 2 percent increase in the national consumer price index.

The bank monitors exchange rates very closely because excessive strength in the exchange rate for the Swiss franc can cause inflation. The franc's exchange rate can rise rapidly when investors flock to the currency during times of global uncertainty. For this reason, the SNB favors a weak franc and doesn't hesitate to intervene in the foreign exchange market. It also conducts open-market operations to influence its monetary policy.

The SNB publishes a quarterly bulletin that includes a monetary policy report of the policy decisions made by its governing board. In its June annual report, it provides a three-year inflation forecast.

To implement its monetary policy, SNB sets an interest rate target range for the London Interbank Offered Rate (*Libor*) for three-month CHF deposits. The bank supplies more or less funds through *repos* to ensure the Libor rate stays in the target range.

Wealth Builders

You can find out more about the Swiss National Bank's monetary policies at its website: www.snb.ch/e/index3.html. On the Publications page, you can find links to its quarterly and annual reports.

Key characteristics and trends for the Swiss franc include the following:

♦ Funds move into the country during times of international economic stability, so the value of the CHF will appreciate during those periods.

♦ News about Swiss banking changes can negatively affect the Swiss economy and the CHF.

♦ Switzerland is the fourth-largest holder of gold, which is viewed as the ultimate safe haven, and the CHF has

def•i•ni•tion

Repos are repurchase agreements. The SNB uses a type of repo where a financial institution sells securities to the SNB with the promise to repurchase the securities in a set period of time. The **Libor** is a trademark of the British Bank Association and is the most widely used benchmark for short-term interest rates worldwide.

an almost 80 percent positive correlation with gold—when gold appreciates, the CHF appreciates.

◆ The CHF is one of the most popular currencies to sell for carry trades because of its low interest rates.

◆ Watch the interest rate differentials between the euro and the Swiss franc for clues about money flows.

◆ Mergers and acquisitions are common in the Swiss banking and insurance industries and can affect CHF spot prices.

◆ The euro/franc (EUR/CHF) is the most commonly traded currency pair. USD/CHF is less common, less liquid, and more volatile. Only during times of extreme global risk aversion will the USD/CHF develop a market of its own.

United States

The U.S. economy is the largest in the world, with a GDP of US$12.37 trillion, which makes up more than 20 percent of the world's total gross product. The United States has the world's fourth-largest labor force. Its market-based economy is largely service oriented, with approximately 79 percent of its firms in the service section, 20 percent in industry, and 1 percent in agriculture.

The United States imports significantly more than any other country and is the third-largest exporter of goods. Canada is its most important trade partner. Its large trade deficit is US$799.5 billion, which can be explained by the fact that the United States is the largest trading partner for many countries. Its external debt exceeded US$8.84 trillion in 2005, the highest of any country.

Long-term financial risks for the country include insufficient investment in the country's economic infrastructure, rapidly rising medical and pension costs for the aging population, skyrocketing energy costs, the large trade and budget deficits, and the widening gap in family income between the lower- and upper-economic classes.

The central bank for the United States is the Federal Reserve (the Fed), which seeks to promote maximum employment, stability in the purchasing power of the dollar, and moderate long-term interest rates. It is an independent entity within the government that does not need presidential approval for its actions, but is under the regulatory supervision of the Congress.

The Fed's Federal Open Market Committee (FOMC) oversees market operations. The FOMC holds eight annual meetings at which interest rate changes and economic expectations are announced. The FOMC forecasts GDP growth, inflation, and unemployment rates. The Fed releases a biannual Monetary Policy Report in February and July.

One way the Fed manages monetary policy is through open-market operations, which include selling government securities based on projections of the supply and demand of Federal Reserve balances. When the Fed purchases securities, interest rates decrease; when it sells securities, interest rates increase.

The Fed also sets the federal funds rate target, which is the interest rate for funds that the Fed loans to other banks. This interest rate impacts all other types of interest rates, including rates for mortgages and consumer loans.

The U.S. Treasury gives instructions regarding whether the Fed should intervene in the foreign exchange markets. The U.S. Treasury may request that the Fed buy or sell the USD, depending upon whether it believes the dollar is over- or undervalued. The New York Federal Reserve Bank carries out all foreign exchange interventions.

Key characteristics and trends for the United States dollar include the following:

 **Wealth Builders**

You can find out more about the New York Fed and its foreign exchange activities at www.newyorkfed.org/education/fx/foreign.html. You can find out more about the Federal Reserve and its monetary policies at www.federalreserve.gov.

- ◆ The USD is the currency used most often in international transactions and constitutes more than half of other countries' official reserves.

- ◆ Many emerging-market countries peg their local currency rates to the USD.

- ◆ Gold is measured in USD, so gold and the USD tend to have inverse relationships.

◆ There is a strong positive correlation between the U.S. stock and bond markets and the USD.

◆ U.S. economic policymakers favor a strong dollar.

◆ Interest rate differentiation between U.S. Treasury bonds and foreign bonds are a strong indicator of potential currency movements.

The Least You Need to Know

◆ You should learn as much as you can about the economic and monetary policies of any country whose currency you want to trade. Be sure you know how to find out more information about the monetary policies and follow any announcements or reports from the entity managing that country's currency.

◆ The currencies of all the industrial countries considered to have less risk for foreign currency exchange transactions are managed by strong central banks.

◆ If you want to trade currencies, be sure you know which currency pairs are the most liquid.

◆ Get to know the politics of the countries whose currency you trade, as well as who sets monetary policy for those countries.

Chapter 7

Taking More Risks— Emerging Country Currencies

In This Chapter

- Understanding emerging markets
- Reviewing riskier country currencies
- Exploring liquidity concerns
- Discovering emerging markets with potential

After you've been trading for a while, you may want to try taking on more risk for the possibility of greater financial rewards. You can do that with more volatile emerging country currencies, but beware. Be certain the money you risk is money you can afford to lose.

Emerging country currencies are not only more risky and volatile, they can also be less liquid—meaning you may not be able to buy or sell them at the price you want because there may not be buyers or sellers for that currency pair. Some of these currencies are sold on the spot market, but many are not. We detail this as we discuss each country's currency.

This chapter briefly discusses what we consider to be the best potential emerging country currencies (at the time this was written) that you may want to consider. Before getting started, be sure you conduct your own intensive research about the countries and their currencies before you trade.

Wealth Builders

If you want to trade the currencies from emerging countries, you need to know about the political conditions and economy of the countries. One good source is the Background Notes prepared by the U.S. State Department on its website at www.state.gov/r/pa/ ei/bgn. Co-author Gary Tilkin provides up-to-date information about the emerging countries' currencies on his company's website at www. gftforex.com/resources/currency/emerging.asp. Another good source for country information is the World Factbook (www.odci.gov/cia/ publications/factbook).

China

China is by far the largest emerging country; and its currency, the Chinese renminbi (RMB), commonly known as yuan, may grow into a more dominant player in years to come. But before jumping on the RMB bandwagon, be sure you understand that China is a Communist Party-led state, which means the state is still very much in control even though it is dabbling in economic reform and opening its markets.

The Communist Party leadership could change, and new Chinese Communist Party leaders could reverse all gains that were made in the past 10 to 20 years. The Chinese Communist Party has 66.35 million members. China does have eight minor parties, but they are all under Communist supervision.

China's 2005 GDP was US$2.26 trillion, which sounds large, but its per-capita GDP is only US$1,700 compared to US$30,000 to US$40,000 in the developed industrial countries. China's GDP is growing rapidly. The growth rate in 2005 was 9.9 percent, driven primarily by China's decision to put greater emphasis on developing a consumer demand-driven economy to sustain economic growth and address global trade imbalances.

China has many exports. Its natural resources include coal, iron ore, crude oil, mercury, tin, tungsten, antimony, manganese, molybdenum, vanadium, magnetite, aluminum, lead, zinc, and uranium. China also has the world's largest potential for hydropower. Its farmers are among the world's largest producers of rice, wheat, potatoes, corn, peanuts, tea, millet, and barley. Their commercial crops include cotton, fibers, apples, oilseeds, pork, and fish. China also produces a variety of live-stock products.

Chinese industry is growing rapidly, too, and includes mining and ore processing, iron, steel, aluminum, coal, machinery, textiles, apparel, armaments, petroleum, cement, chemicals, fertilizers, consumer prod-ucts (such as footwear, toys, and electronics), automobiles and other transportation equipment (such as rail cars, locomotives, ships, and air-craft), and telecommunications products.

China is firmly committed to economic reform and opening to the out-side world. Reform of state industries and the establishment of a social safety network are the two top government priorities named by China's leaders. The government plans to privatize unprofitable state-owned enterprises and develop a pension system for workers. China's leader-ship has also downsized the government bureaucracy.

The next five years will be a critical period in China's development. To investors and firms, China represents a vast market that has yet to be fully tapped and a low-cost base for export-oriented production. China is also partnering with foreign universities, which has helped to create new research and educational opportunities for its students.

China plans to showcase its development gains over the past two decades to the world as they host the 2008 Summer Olympics.

China's economy grew at an average rate of 10 percent per year dur-ing the period from 1990 to 2004, the highest growth rate in the world. China's total trade in 2005 surpassed US$1.4 trillion, making China the world's third-largest trading nation after the United States and Germany. Such high growth is necessary if China is to generate the 15 million jobs needed annually—roughly the size of Ecuador or Cambodia—for new entrants into the job market.

Chinese exports totaled US$762.3 billion in 2005, including trade in electronics; machinery; apparel; optical, photographic, and medical equipment; and furniture. Its main export trading partners include the United States, Hong Kong, Japan, the EU, South Korea, and Singapore. China imported US$660.2 billion worth of products in 2005 in electronics, machinery, petroleum products, chemicals, and steel. China's main import trading partners are Japan, the EU, Taiwan, South Korea, the United States, and Hong Kong.

Serious imbalances exist behind the spectacular trade performance, high investment flows, and high GDP growth. High numbers of non-performing loans weigh down the state-run banking system. Inefficient state-owned enterprises are still a drag on growth, despite announced efforts to sell, merge, or close the vast majority of the inefficient enterprises.

The United States is one of China's primary suppliers of power-generating equipment, aircrafts and parts, computers and industrial machinery, raw materials, and chemical and agricultural products. However, U.S. exporters continue to have concerns about fair market access. In addition, a lack of transparency in the regulatory process makes it difficult for businesses to plan for changes in the domestic market structure.

Conditions are improving for business between the United States and China. On April 11, 2006, the United States-China Joint Commission on Commerce and Trade (JCCT) produced agreements on key U.S. trade concerns ranging from market access to U.S. beef, medical devices, and telecommunications to the enforcement of intellectual property rights, including computer software. The JCCT also produced an agreement to establish a U.S.-China High Technology and Strategic Trade Working Group to review export control cooperation and facilitate high-technology trade.

The USD/RMB is the most liquid currency pair involving the RMB, but the average trading volume is still small—only US$200 million; so if you buy USD/RMB, you may not be able to sell the pair quickly. From 1994 until mid-2005, the RMB was pegged to the U.S. dollar. In mid-2005, China removed the USD peg and it is now pegged to a basket of currencies dominated by the U.S. dollar, the euro, and the yen, but it still is not allowed to float in value and it is not traded openly on the *spot Forex market.*

China must continue its economic reforms and strengthen its banking systems before spot trading can begin, which means the currency will not be available for spot trading for a while. There is no forward market, which means you cannot buy a contract that will allow you to trade the currency at a future date. The bond market is restricted to designated onshore financial institutions and is not liquid.

def•i•ni•tion

A **spot Forex market** is one in which the currency is bought and sold for cash and delivered immediately.

Czech Republic

After the collapse of the Soviet Union, the Czech Republic emerged as one of the most stable and prosperous post-Communist countries, but a currency crisis in the late 1990s set back its march to develop its economy. The country's account deficit was so large that there were fears that its currency, the Czech koruna (CZK), would become unsustainable.

The central bank of the Czech Republic tried unsuccessfully to boost the currency by spending US$3 billion. When that effort failed, the Czech government established a restructuring program that encouraged the sale of firms to foreign countries. This resulted in strong growth boosted by exports and strong recoveries in foreign and domestic investments. Its admission to the European Union in 2004 also spurred growth and structural reform.

The Czech Republic, which runs under the parliamentary system of government, was established on January 1, 1993. Its exports in 2005 totaled US$79 billion, including motor vehicles, machinery, iron, steel, chemicals, raw materials, and consumer goods. The Czech Republic imported about US$78 billion in goods. Its primary trading partner is Germany, but it also trades with Slovakia, Poland,

Wealth Builders

You can follow news about the efforts to strengthen the Czech koruna at the website of the Czech National Bank— www.cnb.cz/en/index.html. You will also find information about the country's monetary policy on that website.

France, Austria, Italy, the Netherlands, Russia, the United Kingdom, China, and the United States. The Czech Republic plans to adopt the euro in 2010.

The Czech Republic has made significant progress toward creating a stable and attractive climate for investment, although continuing reports of corruption are troubling to investors. The country's economic success allowed it to become the first post-Communist country to receive an investment-grade credit rating by international credit institutions. Successive Czech governments have welcomed U.S. investment, in addition to the strong economic influence of Western Europe and increasing investment from Asian auto manufacturers. Inflows of foreign direct investment in 2005 were US$10 billion, doubling the previous year's total. By U.S. embassy estimates, the United States is among the top five investors in the Czech Republic since the revolution in 1989.

The Czech Republic boasts a flourishing consumer production sector. In the early 1990s, most state-owned industries were privatized through a voucher privatization system. Every citizen was given the opportunity to buy, for a moderate price, a book of vouchers that he or she could exchange for shares in state-owned companies. State ownership of businesses was estimated to be about 97 percent under communism. The nonprivate sector is less than 20 percent Communist-owned today.

The economy grew by 4.8 percent in 2005 and should see similar growth in 2006. The government has committed itself to reducing the deficit to 3 percent of GDP by 2008 to meet the requirements for adoption of the euro, and has taken some steps to reduce expenditures and raise revenues. The Czech Republic became a European Union member on May 1, 2004. Most barriers to trade in industrial goods with the EU fell in the course of the accession process to EU membership, which had a positive impact on reform in the Czech Republic. EU directives and regulations shape the Republic's current business environment.

The Czech Republic's economic transformation is not yet complete. The government still faces serious challenges in completing industrial restructuring, increasing transparency in capital market transactions, transforming the housing sector, and reforming the pension and health-care systems.

Foreign investors have unrestricted access to the local markets. The banks of London are very active in the Czech Republic's currency market and account for more than half of the daily turnover of its currency. The deposit market is very liquid, and foreign investors are very active. The euro/koruna is the most commonly traded currency pair involving the koruna, with a daily trading volume of € 2 to 3 billion.

Hong Kong

Hong Kong became a Special Administrative Region of the People's Republic of China in 1997 after 150 years of British rule, yet it does enjoy a high degree of autonomy in all matters except foreign and defense affairs.

The Sino-British Joint Declaration (1984) guarantees that Hong Kong will retain its political, economic, and judicial systems, as well as its unique way of life, for 50 years. In the past year and a half, the Communist government of China has taken a more active role in overseeing the Hong Kong government's management of political developments in the Special Administrative Region. Although Hong Kong remains a free and open society, some in Hong Kong have alleged manipulation or pressure during the 2004 Legislative Council election.

Hong Kong is one of the world's most open and dynamic economies. Its per-capita GDP is comparable to other developed countries. Real GDP expanded by 8.2 percent in 2004, driven by thriving exports, vibrant inbound tourism, and strong pickup of consumer spending. Hong Kong experienced deflation from November 1998 until July 2004, when inflation reappeared at a 0.9 percent rate, measured year on year. A slack property market has also contributed significantly to deflation. By mid-2003, property prices had fallen 66 percent from their late-1997 peak, but have since rebounded by about 58 percent from that lower base. The Hong Kong government has generally resisted pressure for large-scale public expenditures to stimulate the economy because of growing public policy concerns with the government budget deficit.

Hong Kong enjoys a number of economic strengths, including accumulated public and private wealth from decades of unprecedented growth, a sound banking system, virtually no public debt, a strong legal system, and an able and rigorously enforced anticorruption regime.

Hong Kong wants to improve its attractiveness as a commercial and trading center, especially in its position as a gateway to China. These efforts include the conclusion of a free-trade agreement with China, which applies zero tariffs to all Hong Kong-origin goods and preferential treatment in 27 service sectors. U.S. companies have a generally favorable view of Hong Kong's business environment, including its legal system and the free flow of information, low taxation, and infrastructure.

The American Chamber of Commerce's annual business confidence survey, released in December 2005, showed 98 percent of respondents had a "good" or "satisfactory" outlook for 2006. Survey results indicated a positive economic outlook through 2008.

The Hong Kong dollar (HKD) is pegged to the U.S. dollar. A bank can only issue the HKD if it has the same amount of USD on deposit. In 2005, the upper and lower interest rates were adjusted to narrow the interest rate gap between Hong Kong and the United States. Decisions about Hong Kong's currency is managed by a currency board system run by the Hong Kong Monetary Authority.

Wealth Builders

You can get the latest news about Hong Kong monetary policy at the Hong Kong Monetary Authority website: www.info.gov.hk/hkma/eng/currency/link_ex/index.htm. You can also read more about how a currency board system works.

There is no distinction between local and offshore trading. There are no spot or forward trading restrictions, but documentation is required. There is a liquid government bond market (Exchange Fund Notes) with maturities of up to 10 years. Interest rate swaps and options are liquid up to 10 years.

The most liquid currency pair involving the HKD is USD/HKD. The average daily trading volume for the HKD is US$1.5 billion.

Hungary

Under the slogan "economic patriotism," the government moved to increase its role in the economy and switch from an export-driven to a domestic demand-driven economy in the late 1990s. The current government is focused on deficit reduction so that it can meet its goal of joining the Euro Zone by 2010. Its large fiscal deficit is its biggest barrier to success for that goal.

EU countries are its primary trading partners, with Germany as its most important trading partner. The United States has become Hungary's sixth-largest export market, whereas Hungary is ranked only as the seventy-second-largest export market for the United States.

Hungary exported US$58.2 billion in 2004, including machinery, vehicles, food, beverages, tobacco, crude oil, raw materials, manufactured goods, fuels, and electric energy. It imported US$63.2 billion worth of products, including machinery, vehicles, manufactured goods, fuels and electric energy, food, beverages, and tobacco.

Foreign investment was the key to Hungary's success. With about US$55.44 billion in foreign investment since 1989, more than US$15.2 billion has come from U.S. companies. The largest U.S. investors include GE, Alcoa, General Motors, Coca-Cola, Ford, IBM, and PepsiCo. Foreign companies modernized Hungary's industrial sector and created thousands of new high-skilled and high-paying jobs. Foreign companies account for more than 70 percent of Hungary's exports, 33 percent of its GDP, and about one quarter of new jobs. Its GDP in 2004 was US$101.5 billion.

The relatively high value of Hungary's currency, the Hungarian forint (HUF), has put its export-oriented industry at a disadvantage against foreign competitors with lower-valued currencies. The HUF is a fully convertible and a generally floating currency, but its trading volume each day is only € 500 to € 700 million.

Hungary plans to phase out the forint from 2010 to 2012, but some question whether Hungary can meet this goal because its inflation rates and foreign debt are high.

India

Many expect India's currency, the Indian rupee (INR), to become the first of the emerging markets to become spot eligible without restrictions and documentation. Similar to the United States, India has a federal form of government, but the central government in India has greater power in relation to its states. It has also adopted the British-style parliamentary system.

The government exercises its broad administrative powers in the name of the president, but the real national executive power is centered in the Council of Ministers (its Cabinet), led by the prime minister. The president appoints the prime minister, who is designated by legislators of the political party or coalition that holds the largest parliamentary majority in its lower house (*Lok Sabha*). The president then appoints subordinate ministers on the advice of the prime minister.

India's 2004 GDP was US$691 billion, with a growth rate of 6.9 percent, which translates into a per-capita GDP of only US$640. Its exports in 2004 totaled US$76.3 billion, including agricultural products, engineering goods, precious stones, cotton apparel and fabrics, gems and jewelry, handicrafts, and tea. Its imports totaled US$99.8 billion, including petroleum, machinery and transport equipment, electronic goods, edible oils, fertilizers, chemicals, gold, textiles, iron, and steel. India's major trade partners include the United States, the EU, Russia, and Japan.

def•i•ni•tion

A **managed float regime,** also known as a "dirty float," is one in which the exchange rates fluctuate from day to day, but a central bank attempts to influence the country's exchange rates by buying and selling currencies.

The Indian rupee is managed by the Reserve Bank of India and is classified as a *managed float regime.* Documentation is needed for offshore trading.

India does have a very liquid bond market with maturities of up to 25 years available because the government does need to fund a substantial budget deficit. The most liquid currency pair is the USD/INR, but average daily trading volume is just US$750 million.

Korea

The Republic of Korea (South Korea) has experienced phenomenal growth over the past 30 years. Its per-capita GNP climbed from just US$100 in 1963 to US$14,000 in 2004. South Korea is the United

States' seventh-largest trading partner and commands the eleventh-largest economy in the world.

South Korea is a republic with powers shared between the presidency, the legislature, and the judiciary. The president is chief of state and is elected for a single term of five years.

In the past few years, South Korea's economic growth potential fell due to structural problems as well as a rapidly aging population. One of the biggest concerns is South Korea's rigid labor regulations and the need for more constructive relations between management and workers. Other key concerns are the country's underdeveloped financial markets and a general lack of regulatory transparency. Korea also needs to restructure its conglomerates (*chaebols*) and create a better mechanism that will make it easier for bankrupt firms to exit the market. Korean policymakers are increasingly worried about diversion of corporate investment to China and other lower-wage countries.

Korea's GDP in 2005 was US$811.1 billion. Its exports totaled US$284.6 billion, including electronic products (semiconductors, cellular phones, and computers), automobiles, machinery and equipment, steel, ships, and textiles. Korea imported US$261.1 billion, including crude oil, food, machinery and transportation equipment, chemicals and chemical products, and base metals. Its major trading partners include China, the United States, the EU, and Japan.

The Korean won (KRW) is a floating currency, but local and offshore markets are treated separately. Documentation is required for delivery at maturity. The most liquid currency pair involving the KRW is the USD/KRW. Trading volume is about US$2 billion daily.

Mexico

Mexico's economy is highly dependent on exports to the United States, which account for almost a quarter of the country's GDP, so its economy is strongly linked to the ups and downs of the U.S. business cycle. The United States buys about 88 percent of Mexico's exports, including petroleum, cars, and electronic equipment. Mexico's trade policy is among the most open in the world, which includes free-trade agreements with the United States, Canada, the EU, and many other countries.

Mexico's economic stability improved dramatically after the devaluation of Mexico's currency, the Mexican peso (MXN), in 1994. In 2004, the key bond rating companies issued investment-grade ratings for Mexico's debt.

One of Mexico's biggest assets is its oil industry. Mexico is the world's fifth-largest producer of oil and the ninth-largest oil exporter. It is also the United States' third-largest supplier of oil. Oil and gas revenues provide about one third of all Mexican government revenues. The state owns the oil company Pemex, which holds a constitutionally established monopoly for the exploration, production, transportation, and marketing of the nation's oil. The Mexican government is a republic with a president as a chief of state, as well as a legislative and judicial branch.

Mexico's foreign exchange and local debt markets are very liquid. The government on a weekly basis issues bills with terms ranging from one month up to one year. It also issues longer-term debt with terms of up to five years, but the shorter-term bills are more liquid.

The most commonly traded currency pairs are the USD/MXN and the EUR/MXN. The average daily trading volume is US$7 billion.

Poland

Poland's investment-friendly climate helped the country attract more than US$85 billion in direct foreign investment since 1990, with roughly US$7 billion in 2004 alone. Poland is tied with Germany as the most attractive destination for foreign investment in Europe, according to an Ernst and Young report.

Foreign investors are attracted to Poland because of the availability of cheap land and a large, relatively skilled labor force. One of the barriers to even greater success is that the government continues to play a strong role in the economy, as seen in excessive red tape and a high level of politicization in many business decisions.

Investors complain that state regulation is not transparent or predictable, and the economy suffers from a lack of competition in many sectors, notably telecommunications. The Polish government is a republic with a president as head of state, a legislative branch, and a judicial branch.

Poland's GDP in 2004 was US$244 billion. Its exports totaled US$80.9 billion, including furniture, cards, ships, coal, and apparel. Its imports totaled US$87.1 billion, including crude oil, passenger cars, pharmaceuticals, car parts, and computers.

The United States and other Western countries helped to support Poland's growth of a free-enterprise economy by reducing Poland's foreign debt burden in the 1990s, and by providing economic aid and lowering trade barriers. Poland officially joined the EU in 2004. It had planned to convert its currency, the Polish zloty (PLN), to the euro in 2008, but the government extended that deadline to at least 2010 because economic conditions do not yet meet requirements.

The Polish zloty has been a floating currency since 2000. Most money market transactions are conducted through foreign exchange swaps for offshore investors. The most liquid currency pairs for the PLN are the USD/PLN and the EUR/PLN. The average daily trading volume is US$1 billion.

Singapore

Singapore's strategic location on major sea lanes and its industrious population give the country an economic importance in Southeast Asia disproportionate to its small size. In 2004, the economy expanded by 8.4 percent, driven by the growth in world electronics demand, especially in the economies of its major trading partners, the United States, the EU, China, and Japan.

Singapore's government is largely corruption-free. It also boasts a skilled workforce and an advanced and efficient infrastructure, which has attracted investors from more than 7,000 multinational corporations based in the United States, Japan, and Europe. Foreign firms can be found in almost all sectors of the economy. Multinational corporations account for more than two thirds of manufacturing output and direct export sales, although certain services sectors remain dominated by government-linked companies. The electronics industry leads Singapore's manufacturing sector, accounting for 40 percent of Singapore's total industrial output. The industries with the greatest future potential are the chemical and biomedical/pharmaceutical industries, whose development is prioritized by the government.

Singapore's rising wages are a threat to its competitive position, so the government promotes higher value-added activities in the manufacturing and services sectors. It opened its financial services, telecommunications, and power-generation and retailing sectors to foreign service providers and greater competition. The government also pursued cost-cutting measures, including tax cuts and wage and rent reductions, to lower the cost of doing business in Singapore.

The United States leads in foreign investment, accounting for 33 percent of new commitments to the manufacturing sector in 2004. As of 2003, the stock of investment by U.S. companies in the manufacturing and services sectors in Singapore reached about US$61.4 billion. The bulk of U.S. investment is in electronics manufacturing, oil refining and storage, and the chemical industry. More than 1,500 U.S. firms operate in Singapore.

Singapore's total trade in 2004 amounted to US$354 billion, an increase of 27 percent from 2003. Singapore is the fifteenth-largest trading partner of the United States. Malaysia and the United States are Singapore's two top trading partners. Singapore's principal exports are petroleum products, food and beverages, chemicals, textile and garments, electronic components, telecommunication apparatus, and transport equipment. Singapore's main imports are aircraft, crude oil and petroleum products, electronic components, consumer electronics, microelectronics manufacturing equipment, motor vehicles, chemicals, food and beverages, iron and steel, and textile yarns and fabrics.

Singapore has a parliamentary republic with a president as chief of state and a prime minister as head of the government. It also has legislative and judicial branches.

The Monetary Authority of Singapore, a government agency, manages the Singapore dollar (SGD) using a managed float regime. The Monetary Authority seeks to reduce import inflation and to balance demand. There are no local or offshore restrictions, so documentation is not required to trade the currency. There is a liquid spot market and a limited forward foreign exchange market. Both the government and the corporate bond markets have grown in popularity in recent years. The most liquid currency pair involving the SGD is the USD/SGD. The SGD's average daily trading volume is US$1 billion.

South Africa

South Africa has a two-tiered economy: one that rivals other developed countries and the other with only the most basic infrastructure. This results in uneven distribution of wealth and income, which was primarily caused by apartheid. The country's transition to a democratic, non-racial government began in early 1990.

Some parts of South Africa include productive and industrialized economies that exhibit many characteristics associated with developing countries, including mining, manufacturing, services, and agriculture sectors. South Africa's key challenge is to achieve sustained economic growth while at the same time addressing the socioeconomic disparities created by apartheid.

The government of South Africa demonstrated its commitment to open markets, privatization, and a favorable investment climate, but its wealth remains very unequally distributed along racial lines. However, South Africa's budgetary reforms that aim at better reporting, auditing, and increased accountability, and the structural changes to its monetary policy framework, including inflation targeting, have created transparency and predictability and are widely acclaimed. Trade liberalization has been a primary goal since the early 1990s. South Africa has reduced its import-weighted average tariff rate from more than 20 percent in 1994 to 7 percent in 2002. South Africa is moving toward the acceptance of free-market principles.

South Africa has a sophisticated financial structure with a large and active stock exchange that ranks seventeenth in the world in terms of total market capitalization.

The South African Reserve Bank (SARB) performs all central banking functions. The SARB is independent and operates similarly to Western central banks, influencing interest rates and controlling liquidity of its currency, the South African rand (ZAR), through its interest rates on funds provided to private sector banks.

> **Wealth Builders**
>
> You can find out more about the South African Reserve Bank at www.resbank.co.za/navigate.htm. You can also find economic news and more about South Africa's monetary policy.

The South African government has taken steps to gradually reduce remaining foreign exchange controls, which apply only to South African residents. Private citizens are now allowed a one-time investment of up to 750,000 rand in offshore accounts. Since 2001, South African companies have been allowed to invest up to ZAR750 million in Africa and ZAR500 million elsewhere. The South African government is a parliamentary democracy with a president as chief of state, a legislative branch, and a judicial branch.

South Africa has rich mineral resources. It is the world's largest producer and exporter of gold and platinum and also exports a significant amount of coal. During 2000, platinum overtook gold as South Africa's largest foreign exchange earner. Its GDP was US$213 billion in 2004. Trade exports totaled US$36.3 billion, including gold, other minerals and metals, agricultural products, and motor vehicles and parts. Imports totaled US$34 billion, including machinery, transport equipment, chemicals, petroleum products, textiles, and scientific instruments. Its trading partners include the United Kingdom, the United States, Germany, Italy, Japan, and Eastern Asia.

South Africa's foreign exchange and money markets are liquid, with active participation from onshore and offshore investors. The bond market also is well developed with a term structure of 30 years. There are restrictions for offshore investors, but these are rarely enforced.

Thailand

The Thai economy is export-dependent, with exports accounting for 60 percent of GDP, which was US$163.2 billion in 2004. Its government is a constitutional monarchy with a king as head of state and a prime minister as head of the government, which does include legislative and judicial branches.

The Royal Thai government welcomes foreign investment. Investors who are willing to meet certain requirements can apply for special investment privileges through the Board of Investment. Roughly 60 percent of Thailand's labor force is employed in agriculture. Rice is the country's most important crop. Other agricultural commodities produced in significant amounts include fish and fishery products, tapioca, rubber, corn, and sugar. Exports of processed foods such as canned tuna, pineapples, and frozen shrimp are on the rise.

Thailand's diversified manufacturing sector contributed the greatest share of the country's growth in the past 10 years. Industries with rapid increases in production include computers and electronics, garments and footwear, furniture, wood products, canned food, toys, plastic products, gems, and jewelry. High-technology products such as integrated circuits and parts, electrical appliances, and vehicles are now leading Thailand's strong growth in exports.

The United States is Thailand's largest export market and second-largest supplier, after Japan. Thailand's major markets are North America, Japan, and Europe. Machinery and parts, vehicles, electronic integrated circuits, chemicals, crude oil and fuels, and iron and steel are among Thailand's principal imports.

Although the economy has demonstrated moderate positive growth since 1999, future performance depends on continued reform of the financial sector, corporate debt restructuring, attracting foreign investment, and increasing exports. Telecommunications, roadways, electricity generation, and ports have shown increasing strain during the country's period of sustained economic growth and may pose a future challenge. Thailand's growing shortage of engineers and skilled technical personnel may limit its future technological creativity and productivity.

Thailand's currency, the Thai baht (THB), is a freely floating currency with segregated domestic and offshore markets. Official documentation is required to trade the baht in the spot and forward markets. The government bond market has grown rapidly since 1997, helping to build the corporate bond market, which is now flourishing. The most liquid currency pair including the THB is the USD/THB. The baht's daily trading volume averages US$700 to US$900 million.

Turkey

Turkey is a large, middle-income country with relatively few mineral resources. Its economy is currently in transition from a high degree of reliance on agriculture and heavy industrial economy to a more diverse, more modern economy with an increasingly important and globalized services sector. Turkey's economy suffered from high inflation for 30 years, from the early 1970s until the current reform period. Coming out of a tradition of a state-directed economy that was relatively closed to the outside world, Turkey's government leaders began to open up the economy in the 1980s. In the 1990s, Turkey's economy suffered from a series of coalition governments with weak economic policies, leading to boom-and-bust cycles culminating in a severe banking and economic crisis in 2001 and a deep economic downturn that increased unemployment.

Since the crisis, however, Turkey's economy has recovered strongly thanks to good monetary and fiscal policies and structural economic reforms made with the support of the International Monetary Fund and the World Bank. The independence of Turkey's Central Bank from political interference has been firmly established. The bank manages a floating exchange rate system for Turkey's currency, the Turkish lira (TRL). In addition, there have been substantial reforms in the financial, energy, and telecommunications sectors that have included the privatization of several large state-owned institutions.

Wealth Builders

You can find out more about Turkey's monetary policy at the website of the Central Bank of the Republic of Turkey: www. tcmb.gov.tr/yeni/eng/index. html. There you can also find key interest rates and foreign exchange rates.

After years of low-level foreign direct investment, in 2005 Turkey succeeded in attracting US$9.6 billion and expects a similar level in 2006. A series of large privatizations, the stability fostered by the start of Turkey's EU accession negotiations, strong and stable growth, and structural changes in the banking, retail, and telecommunications sectors have all contributed to the rise in foreign investment. Turkey has taken steps to improve its investment climate through administrative streamlining and an end to foreign investment screening. It also strengthened intellectual property legislation. However, a number of disputes involving foreign investors in Turkey and certain policies, such as high taxation of cola products and continuing gaps in the intellectual property regime, inhibit investment.

The Turkish government is a republic with a president as chief of state and a prime minister as head of the government. It also has legislative and judicial branches. Its exports totaled US$63.1 billion in 2004, including textiles and apparel, iron and steel, electronics, tobacco, and motor vehicles. Imports totaled US$116 billion in 2005, including petroleum, machinery, motor vehicles, electronics, iron and steel, and plastics. Its major trading partners are Germany, the United States, France, Russia, Italy, Japan, the Netherlands, and the United Kingdom.

The Turkish lira is fully convertible, and there are no restrictions on offshore investment in the currency. Both foreign exchange and bond markets are liquid, and offshore investors are fairly active in all markets. The longest maturity for Turkish lira futures is 18 months, but it is most liquid up to 1 year. The most liquid currency pair for the TRL is the USD/TRL, and the lira's daily trading volume averages about US$500 million.

The Least You Need to Know

- Be sure you understand the emerging country's political structure as well as its economic structure before trading the currency.

- Not all emerging country currencies are currently available to trade in spot Forex. Some are available only as currency swaps or futures.

- Research to find out who in the emerging country manages its foreign exchange and how openly that foreign exchange is managed.

- Many emerging-market currencies are not allowed to float, but instead are managed more carefully by government intervention, known as a managed float.

Part 3

Trading Basics

Trading foreign exchange requires learning some new basic tools, as well as using some other basic tools in different ways. In this part, we introduce you to the key trading platforms and software. We also discuss how you can use technical and fundamental analysis to improve your trading potential. And, of course, we can't forget the risks. We explore all the types of risks you must understand when you trade foreign currency.

Chapter 8

Trading Platforms, Hardware, and Software

In This Chapter

- ◆ Determining computer specs
- ◆ Getting connected
- ◆ Finding platforms

Forex trading used to be the province solely of banks, multinational corporations, and hedge funds. Just 10 years ago, most banks closely guarded Forex information, making it difficult to determine exchange rates. This led to an inefficient market where the bid and ask spreads were wide and the costs of trading Forex were high.

Today that is no longer true. Anyone, whether in a small rural U.S. town or in a major European financial center, can trade Forex as long as he or she has a basic computer workstation and a high-speed Internet connection. By picking a reputable Forex firm, you can find a retail platform that gives you the pricing and execution comparable to the interbank market. This chapter discusses your computer hardware and software needs and what to look for in trading platforms.

Computer Hardware and Software Needs

If you're planning to trade Forex, you definitely need a high-performance computer that can run trading software. This software consumes considerable amounts of system resources. Good trading platforms require the ability to test trading strategies and use multiple charts. You must use a multi-window environment and possibly more than one monitor.

A computer with a Windows XP operating system is best because most trading platforms are designed to work on Windows. Although there are trading systems out there that can work on the Apple OS/2 operating system and Linux, you may have some difficulty finding them and finding software that is the most up-to-date.

Here are the basics for the ideal computer workstation:

◆ **Central processing unit (CPU).** Your processor speed should be at a minimum 1 GHz. Trading programs do rely on the ability to make many mathematical calculations, so you should select either an Intel Core or Pentium or AMD Athlon processor. Avoid using Intel Celeron or AMD Duron chips, because they cannot handle these high-demand applications. Most modern computers have enough CPU horsepower to run the trading software you need, but some high-end software could require even specialty hardware, such as multi-CPU and hyperthreading configurations. When choosing a trading platform, read the CPU requirements and make sure you have the hardware to support it.

◆ **RAM memory.** You should have at a minimum 500MB (megabytes) of RAM, but it is best to have considerably more. You can't have too much RAM, but if you have too little the software will run very slowly. Extra memory is not an expensive upgrade, so don't be cheap about it.

◆ **Disk space.** Although 100MB of free disk space should be enough to run most trading platforms, you'll probably want a lot more to store exchange rate data. We recommend at least 1 GB of free space.

◆ **Operating system.** Your best bet is to pick a system with Windows XP. Although you may find some trading applications that can run on older versions of Windows, the reliability and stability of XP is critical for trading. You don't want your system to crash in the middle of a trade. Crashes happen much more frequently on the older Windows systems.

◆ **Video card.** Your best bet is to choose a computer system with a video card that uses its own video memory rather than one that shares its memory with your RAM. You can squeak by with a video card that has 64MB of video memory, but it is better to get one with 128MB or, even better, 256MB. If you are going to run more than one monitor, 128MB per monitor is suggested.

◆ **Monitor size.** You should have at least a 17-inch monitor. A 19-inch or larger is better because you will likely be running several windows at the same time. The old-fashioned cathode ray tube (CRT) monitor is better for reading price charts and spreadsheets with detailed price data because they are sharper. The liquid crystal display (LCD) monitors tend to blur moving images, which can make it more difficult when you're trying to follow small lines on charts and read small numbers in large spreadsheets.

◆ **Dual-monitor configurations.** Many traders prefer to have more than one monitor. They use one monitor for their charts and a second monitor for everything else. If you do decide to use a dual-monitor configuration, be sure your video cards support the configuration.

◆ **Network interface.** You need either a built-in Ethernet port or an extra Ethernet interface card to access a high-speed Internet connection. We do not recommend trading through a wireless network. Wireless networks are not as secure, and can be affected by cell phones, cordless phones, and a variety of other household items.

◆ **Power supply.** For safety, we do recommend that you get an uninterruptible power supply (UPS). In addition to giving the safety of 30 minutes to a couple of hours of power if your electric power goes out, many also come with protection against a lightning strike. You definitely don't want to lose power in the middle of a trade.

◆ **Security.** You must secure your computer and its data against viruses, worms, and other nasty bugs out there. You also want to be sure to have a firewall that protects any attacks from the World Wide Web to your computer. Norton AntiVirus or McAfee's VirusScan are two good virus-protection alternatives. ZoneAlarm is a good firewall package that monitors your Internet activities and detects any Trojans or worms that are trying to call your computer home. Be sure you keep these security software packages up-to-date because new bugs enter the Internet environment almost every day.

Internet Access

Don't think about trading Forex using the Internet unless you have reliable high-speed access. A dial-up connection will not give you the type of access you need to be able to trade in the fast-paced work of Forex, where exchange rates can change every three seconds.

Your access can be digital subscriber line (DSL) through your telephone provider or cable modem through your cable provider. Some active traders even want more reliability and opt for an expensive T1 line, but that expense is not necessary.

Full-time traders need redundancy, and while a dial-up line is not recommended for trading, we do recommend having a dial-up or alternative Internet connection available and ready to be used in case your primary connection fails. The Internet is an unpredictable network with many carriers trying to work together to provide global communication. There will be issues from time to time with your Internet connection, and you do not want to be in the situation where you have an open trade and your primary Internet connection is down.

Additionally, for added protection, it's best that your backup connection is not provided by the same carrier as your primary connection. For example, if you have high-speed access through your cable provider, then set up a dial-up access account through some other company.

Trading Platforms

Finding the right platform for trading can be a much more difficult choice. You definitely want to find a Forex trading platform that can offer the basics—the ability to buy, sell, and settle currency pairs. But all trading platforms are not created equal. Do your research before picking a trading platform!

As part of your research, be sure to first check out the Forex firm before even trying out their software. If you are using a firm based in the United States, one of the best places for researching a Forex firm is the *National Futures Association (NFA)* at www.nfa.futures.org, which is a self-regulatory body for the futures industry that was given its authority by the *Commodity Futures Trading Commission (CFTC)*.

def•i•ni•tion

The **National Futures Association (NFA)** is the industry-wide, self-regulatory organization for the United States futures industry that develops rules, programs, and services to safeguard market integrity, protect investors, and help its members meet regulatory responsibilities.

The **Commodity Futures Trading Commission (CFTC)** is an independent U.S. agency that regulates the commodity futures and option markets in the United States. It ensures the economic utility of the futures markets by encouraging its competitiveness and efficiency; ensuring its integrity; protecting market participants against manipulation, abusive trading practices, and fraud; and ensuring the financial integrity of the clearing process.

Remember, Forex dealers are not regulated in the same way. Only regulated entities, such as banks, insurance companies, broker dealers, or futures commission merchants that are affiliates of regulated entities can handle Forex trades for retail customers. *The company you trade with should be a bank, a broker dealer (registered with the SEC), or an FCM (registered with the CFTC)*. You learn more about Forex fraud in Chapter 16.

On the NFA site, review the basic broker/firm information section for member companies. You can find out information about the firm's registration status and research whether the broker or firm has been disciplined. You can check out the financial information about all registered Forex dealers at the CFTC website (www.cftc.gov).

You can also check out information about Forex brokers and dealers at forums online, but be careful out there. Not all posters are independent traders, so you need to read these forums regularly and get to know who is posting. Two forums with Forex sections are MoneyTec Traders Community Forum (www.moneytec.com) and Elite Trader (www. elitetrader.com).

The MoneyTec Traders Community Forum is a discussion forum that serves as a resource to help Forex traders become better traders. You can meet fellow traders from around the world and learn more about Forex trading, as well as discuss trading ideas, techniques, and strategies. Elite Trader provides an online community for discussion of not only Forex, but also stock, options, and futures trading. Remember to take the information found on these postings with a grain of salt, and be sure to conduct additional research.

After you've narrowed down your retail platform alternatives, be sure to take them out for a test drive before you decide which one is right for you. All reputable firms allow you to download a demonstration of their software so that you can try out the software on your own computer before you open an account.

After downloading the demo, make sure it's not too complicated to use. Sometimes you'll find the software so overloaded with features that it's not the best choice for you. When a software package is overloaded with options, you'll find that streaming quotes sometimes can be jumpy, updates to your account can be slow, and trying to execute orders can be confusing. You certainly don't want a software package with these problems when you're trying to trade quickly in the Forex market.

The most important feature is the software's navigation. You want to be able to get to where you're going quickly and easily on your computer screen. Although all the bells and whistles and pretty colors may look great, make sure that the extras don't impede your ability to trade efficiently.

Currency Corn

Co-author Gary Tilkin's company, GFT, designed one of the first Forex trading platforms in 1999, and the platform is ranked as one of the best in the market today. Tilkin thought the old system of floor trading was slow and filled with confusion about prices. Customers quickly found that the trading platform GFT designed was far superior because it provided them with almost instantaneous trades. The current version of GFT's software, DealBook® 360, is now available on Global Forex Trading (www.gftforex.com). You can access the software using the CD included with this book.

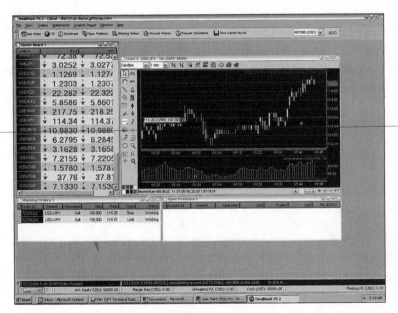

DealBook® 360 Opening Screen.

Key Parts of a Trading Platform

Here are the key pieces of information you want to find on a Forex platform:

◆ **Dealing rates.** You want to locate all available currency pairs for which the dealer can make a market. You want information about how much you can sell a currency pair for and how much you can buy one for (a two-sided quote). You also want to be able to see the highest and lowest prices during the trading period. You want to know the time and date the last quote was posted. Another good feature is to know the interest rates for the currency pair.

- ◆ **Account summary.** You want to have quick access to the status of your account. You need to know your balance (the total amount of capital in your account), the currency pairs you hold, the amount of margin you have used, the amount of margin you have available to use, and your total profit or loss.

- ◆ **Open orders.** You should be able to quickly see what type of order was executed, such as a market or limit order. You learn about order types in Chapter 13. You need to know the currency pair, the price at which the order will be executed, and the size of the trade (or amount of the order). You also want to see any predetermined stop loss or limit orders you set, and the time you entered the order.

- ◆ **Open positions.** You need to know the specific currency pairs you have traded. You need to know the size of each position (amount). You need to know which side of the market you are on (either sell or buy). You need to know the price at which the position was opened. You need to know the current price of your position. You need to know the price at which you entered a stop order. You need to know the price at which you entered a limit order. You need to know the profit or loss of the specific trade. You need to know whether any commissions were charged. You need to know the interest gain or loss on the position.

You may find some additional features in the system you are considering:

- ◆ **Request for quote (RFQ).** This feature enables you to send an instant message within the trading platform to the market maker. You can ask for a quote on a specific currency pair based on the size of the trade you want to make. This process can favor market makers because they're the only ones who see the price. This is an older trading feature and not the preferred method.

- ◆ **ECN.** You will find companies offering an ECN model, which allows multicounterparty trading. Each participant in the network can post bids and offers and trade with each other. The trader can choose the counterparty with which he wants to trade. The name can be deceiving, as these systems don't replicate the ECN model that is known to stock traders. Retail customers must still conduct trades through an intermediary. While brokers using this type of system boast about greater transparency and more competitive pricing, there are often hidden costs or commission fees. Also, sometimes many traders are on the same side of a currency pair and the liquidity is not there for the currency you wish to buy or sell.

◆ **Click and deal.** This is the type of system that is the most common platform for retail Forex traders. It's called click and deal because "what you click is what you get." In basic terms, you click on the trade you want based on the price quote you see. This does increase transparency regarding the deals available and limits the power of the market maker. The quotes you see are live and can be instantly traded upon. In most trading platforms, the prices are streamed, which means that they are continuously updated in real time. This platform is transparent because the market maker must post a two-sided quote—both the buy and sell side. In an RFQ system, the market maker is in control because he can quote the price based on the pair and size the trader requests. Click and deal is well-suited for most retail Forex traders.

For example, in the previous figure, you can see the first screen for GFT's DealBook® 360, which gives you a lot of information. On the left is the quote board, which shows major currency pairs and changes every second as the pricing changes. On the right is the charting feature, which also updates based on the time you set. In the screen shot that follows, we have it set to change every minute, and it shows a chart for USD/JPY (U.S. dollar/Japanese yen). At the bottom of the screen are details for pending orders, but I have no open positions listed. You can see at the bottom of the screen that our account has $50K in working cash. Just to set the record straight, this is not my real money. It's a demonstration account.

In the following figure, you can see how easy it is to place an order using GFT's DealBook® Click and Deal feature. In the New Order box, a drop-down menu gives you all the possible currency pairs you can trade. We're showing you trading pairs

with the U.S. dollar in that drop-down list, but others are available. When you highlight the pair, the bid and ask price shows at
the top of the Order box. You can get a history of price activity
by clicking on that tab or get a quick chart by clicking on that
tab. You can then pick your order type and your order options, as
well as the number of lots you want to sell. When ready, you click
Submit to place the order.

Placing an order with DealBook® 360.

◆ **News.** While the news feature can be a useful addition, it's not
always the best source for information. In many platforms, the
news feature lags the market. By the time you receive the news,
it could already be known by other traders. Seconds can make a
huge difference in Forex trading, where prices can change by the
second. GFT's DealBook® 360 offers real-time streaming news.
This platform even has an RSS feature, allowing you to add whatever streaming news updates you'd like. If you don't have a real-
time news feature, you'll want to supplement it with coverage on a
TV news channel such as Bloomberg or CNBC.

◆ **Charts.** You must have a good charting package. This is critical
for successful traders and should be included with your Forex
software. Charts represent historical price data. You can then

manipulate the data by timescale and period, by currency pairs, and by technical indicators to find your trading opportunity. You learn more about technical analysis and charting in Chapter 9.

◆ **Research.** The research about various currency and currency pairs that you get along with your trading platform is useful, but it's always wise to do your own research and not depend solely on the trading platform you choose for information.

Not every trade will go smoothly. Sometimes glitches will occur. Here are a couple of glitches you should watch out for:

◆ **Requotes.** A requote is when a dealer does not accept the price that you may see on your screen and quotes you a new price. This happens most often when the market is particularly volatile; but if it starts to happen often, watch out. Your dealer could be cheating you and altering quotes in his favor to make more money. If you find your trading platform is resulting in frequent requotes, find a new platform.

◆ **Network connection.** As anyone who's worked on the Internet knows, you can have problems with connectivity. Be sure the trading platform you select has an indicator that you can easily see that lets you know whether the data stream you are seeing is connected. Otherwise you could be making decisions on price quotes that are not the most current.

Retail Forex Trading Platforms

Although of course we are partial to DealBook® 360, which was developed by co-author Gary Tilkin's company GFT, we do think you should do your own research to find the platform that's best for you based not only on the software but also on the currencies that you plan to trade.

DealBook® 360 is available in Chinese, English, French, German, Japanese, Korean, Polish, Portuguese, and Spanish. You need US$250 to open an account. The minimum transaction is US$10,000. That minimum transaction amount is true for all companies listed here. Remember, you only need 1 percent of the transaction amount ($100 in this case) to trade on margin.

In addition to GFT's DealBook® 360, here are some other trading platforms you can try out:

- **Capital Market Services** (www.cmsfx.com)—You can open an account with US$200. Languages available are Arabic, Chinese, English, French, Italian, German, Japanese, Korean, Russian, and Spanish.

- **Forex.com** (www.Forex.com)—You can open a mini account with US$250. Languages available include Chinese, English, and Russian.

- **FX Solutions** (www.fxsol.com)—You can open an account with a minimum of US$250. Languages available are Chinese, English, and Spanish.

- **MG Financial Group** (www.mgforex.com)—You can open an account with a minimum of US$200. Languages include Chinese, English, French, Russian, Spanish, and Urdu.

- **SNC Investments** (www.sncinvestment.com)—You can open an account with a minimum of US$500. Languages available are English, French, Japanese, and Korean.

All companies listed are regulated by the National Futures Association and the Commodity Futures Trading Commission.

The Least You Need to Know

- Be sure you have a computer with the right hardware and software that can handle your trading needs.

- Not all Forex trading platforms are created equal. Try out whatever system you pick by downloading the demo onto your computer and trying it out.

- There are many firms out there. Be sure to choose one that is registered with the National Futures Association and regulated by the NFA and the Commodity Futures Trading Commission.

Chapter 9

Using Technical Analysis

In This Chapter

- ◆ Interpreting charts
- ◆ Noticing trends
- ◆ Finding support
- ◆ Recognizing patterns

Technical analysis looks at the historical price movements of a currency. Technical analysts believe all that needs to be known about a currency can be seen by tracking its historical price, and from that historical data you can spot trends and predict future price movements.

That's very different from fundamental analysts, who look at economic data and other key changes that impact a currency's value to try to predict future price movements. We explore the basics of fundamental analysis in Chapter 10.

In this chapter, we introduce you to the basic types of charts and price patterns, as well as how to recognize trends. You'll need to do a lot of practice and some more study to really be able to master technical analysis. In Appendix C, we recommend books that focus solely on how to use technical analysis in currency trading.

Understanding and Reading Charts

Charts used for technical analysis in Forex trading are like a road map to the historical price movement of a currency. If you took statistics when you were in college, these charts would be known as times series plots.

On the y-axis (vertical axis), you will find the price scale and on the x-axis (horizontal axis), you will find the time scale. Historical prices for the currency are plotted from left to right across the x-axis, with the most recent price shown on the point furthest to the right.

The following is a chart for the U.S. dollar from the charting package included with GFT's DealBook® 360. You can try out this package when you download the software from the CD included with the book. (If you don't have the CD, you can download the DealBook® 360 software at www.gftforex.com.)

You can pick the time periods you want shown on the chart. This chart was set up in one-hour price points, which means each point on the chart represents one hour of trading. Your charting software, which is included with most trading packages, can be set with many different intervals.

When you set the time periods, it compresses the data. A *tick* chart would be the least compressed and a monthly chart would be the most compressed. For example, you may want to see the data intraday, daily, weekly, or monthly. The less compressed the data, the more detail you will see.

def•i•ni•tion

A **tick** chart will change whenever the price changes, which often occurs in less than a minute.

When you pick an interval, the points shown on the table will represent price points during that trading interval. Intervals included on most currency charting software include tick, 1-minute, 5-minute, 10-minute,

15-minute, 20-minute, 25-minute, 30-minute, 35-minute, 40-minute, 45-minute, 50-minute, 55-minute, 1-hour, 2-hour, 4-hour, daily, weekly and monthly.

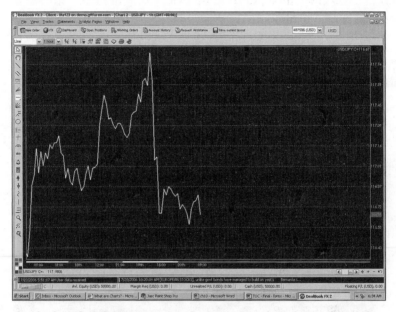

On this basic line chart, you can see the time points along the x-axis and the prices along the y-axis. Price points are plotted from left to right, with the last point on the right being the most recent price.

Currency traders usually concentrate on charts that show intraday data to forecast short-term price movements. Remember the shorter the time frame, the less compressed the data will be. That's when you can see the most detail.

But short-term charts can be volatile and contain a lot of noise, such as sudden price movements and wide high-low ranges, which can distort the overall picture. Try out different time periods using the charting package included on the CD to see how different the picture will be, depending on the time frame you choose. One-hour time periods like in the previous figure are the most commonly used by Forex traders to pick up intraday trends.

Line Chart

The previous figure shows the simplest type of chart called a line chart. This chart is created by plotting one price point of a currency over a specified period of time. The line is made by connecting the dots of each of these plotted points.

Bar Chart

The most popular charting method used by traders is the bar chart (see the following figure). This shows the highs and lows for the currency during the time period selected. Each bar on the chart represents one time period.

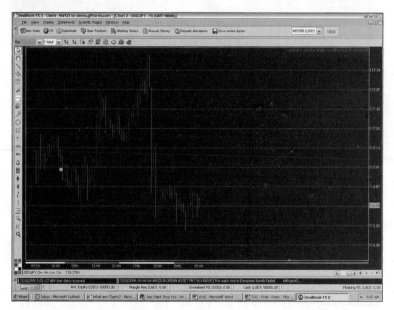

This is a one-hour bar chart for the U.S. dollar. Each bar on the chart shows the high and low trading price for each hour of trading on the chart. This chart was made using GFT's DealBook® 360 software.

Bar charts display a large amount of data. The addition of the high-low range for each time period helps you to recognize the movement between the time periods and more easily pick up the trends. The little lines inside the high-low bar show the opening and closing price for the time period.

Candlestick Chart

Candlestick charts, which originated in Japan over 300 years ago, are regaining popularity among traders. In these charts, instead of just bar lines representing the time periods, you'll see a little box form. The top of the box is the opening price for the period and the bottom of the box is the closing price on a down candle. The opposite is true for an up candle (see the following figure).

On most candlesticks, you'll also see a line above and below the box. The line above the box shows you the high during the period and the line below the box shows you the low.

Candlestick charts show more detail using small boxes to indicate the open and close price for the period. The line above the box shows the high price for the period and the line below the box shows the low price. This chart of the U.S. dollar in one-hour intervals was made using GFT's DealBook® 360.

Many traders find the candlestick charts easier to read, especially when you're trying to judge the relationship between the open and close price. Note that there is a lighter-colored box when the close is higher than the open and a darker-colored box when the close is lower than the open. Officially, the box formed to show the open and close is called the *body*. The lines to show the high and low above and below the body are called *shadows*.

Spotting Trends

You're probably wondering what exactly you're trying to find in all these squiggly lines. You're looking for a trend or a specific pattern for the price movement to attempt to figure out where the price is going and pick good buy and sell points for the currency.

Basically what you can see in these charts is a picture of the psychology of buyers and sellers by looking at the historical price movements. When prices are moving upward, buyers are more interested in buying and sellers are less interested in selling. Conversely, when prices are falling, sellers are more interested in selling to get out before they lose their gains, while buyers are more interested in buying with the hope they can get in at the right price to make a profit on the next upward movement.

Drawing Trend Lines

The first thing you must do is draw a trend line. All you need to do to draw the line is connect two high swings (or peaks) and two low swings (or troughs). I show you the connections in the trend lines that I've drawn in the figure that follows.

As you can see, when you draw a trend line, it's like connecting the dots. You find two points and draw a line between them. On the following chart, you can see an upward trend on the left and a downward trend on the right.

I then expand the chart to a daily chart, which shows the price movement between April and July in the next figure. You can see that the dollar has been on an upward trend since mid-May after seeing a major drop in value from its high on this chart in mid-April.

As a trader, what you want to do is predict which way the dollar is going based on the price history you see in the chart. You determine the trend, upward or downward, and develop a plan to figure out at what point you want to buy and at what point you want to sell the pair.

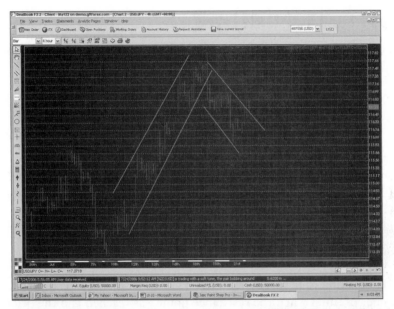

*Trend lines drawn on a four-hour chart for the pair USD/JPY (U.S. dollar/
Japanese yen). The lines were drawn using the charting package included in
the DealBook® 360 software, which is on the CD included with this book.*

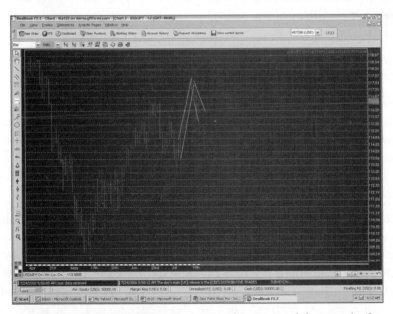

*A daily chart of the USD/JPY pair showing the price trends between April
and July 2006. Note the lines that were drawn using the four-hour chart
to the right of the line appear tiny when you expand the chart for the longer
time frame. The DealBook® 360 charting software was used to draw this
chart.*

Support and Resistance Levels

As you try to make the determination of when to buy or sell a currency, look for signs of support and resistance.

- ◆ Support is a price point below the current market price where buying occurs. It is always the lower trading range boundary. When the price drops to the support level, buyers start to buy because they think the price will rise from this level.

- ◆ Resistance is a price point above the current market price at which sellers decide to sell. It is always the upper trading range boundary. When a currency pair hits the resistance point, buyers are losing interest in buying because the price is too high and sellers must lower their price in order to find buyers.

When reading the chart shown in the previous figure, you can see a number of times when the resistance point was reached and the price for the pair started to head downward. The point to the farthest right shows that when the pair reached a high price of 117.86, it started to drop in value. At that point buyers resisted the price and sellers had to start dropping the price to sell.

You can see that when the pair reached a low 113.44 in early July it proved to be a support point and buyers started buying to stop the price from falling any lower.

You determine these support and resistance points visually by reading your chart. But don't think of charting as an exact science. While I talk about price points as specific numbers to help you learn to read these charts, it's better to think of zones of support and resistance, which translates into buying and selling ranges. Forex traders will see a lot of trading activity around these price points.

What you're trying to locate when you follow trend lines is a breakout point—that's the point when a currency pair drops out of the trading range and heads in the opposite direction. An easy breakout point to spot in the previous figure is in mid-May when the low hits 108.98 after a long drop from the high of 118.82 in mid-April. There you see how an upward trend breaks out and heads back up to 116.60 before it corrects and heads downward again.

Most Forex traders use shorter-term charts to pick up intraday trading signals, but we used this longer-term chart because it is easier to discuss the trends on a less volatile chart. The ups and downs of the market are smoothed out when you look at a longer time frame, so it's easier to see the patterns when you have less detail. You get more detail and the most amount of noise from charts in the shorter time frames, such as 5- or 10-minute charts.

Types of Price Patterns

As you get more experienced working with charting, you'll see that markets follow certain patterns. These patterns become very well known to traders. We review the basics of some of the better-known patterns, but no pattern guarantees you a perfect reading of the future trend for the market.

A well-known phrase among traders is, "the trend is your friend until it ends." When you see a strong trend, try to research the fundamentals behind that trend (see Chapter 10) and you'll have an even better idea of what may be driving that trend and what the next moves for that currency pair might be.

Wedges

The wedge pattern forms when your trend lines look a lot like a symmetrical triangle. You'll see that the trend lines you draw have highs and lows that come together at an angle. Usually this angle points up or down. Then you'll see a trend, either up or down, form outside this pattern. An upward line would be a bullish trend indicating a good time to buy. A downward line would be a bearish trend indicating a good time to sell.

Channels

When you see your trend lines run almost flat with no indication of an upward or downward trend, then what you are seeing is called a channel. This type of pattern indicates that both buyers and sellers are undecided about the direction of the market. When you see this type of pattern, your best bet is to wait until you see signs of a breakout of the market in one direction or the other before picking your buy and sell points.

Gaps

A price gap usually forms when the opening price of the current bar is above or below the closing price of the bar for the previous period. You'll see gaps most often on daily charts, such as the one in the preceding figure. One noticeable gap falls between 5/5 and 5/8, when the close on 5/5 is 112.56 and the open on 5/8 is 112.02. Frequently a gap can be an indication of a more dramatic breakout. In this situation, the pair continued to fall in value.

There are many other types of patterns traders use to determine their buying and selling strategies. We don't have the space in one brief chapter to teach you all the basics of technical trading, but we at least wanted to give you a taste of the possibilities.

The keys to successfully working with charts are dedication, focus, and consistency:

- Dedication: You must decide you want to take the time to learn the basics of chart analysis and then apply this knowledge on a regular basis so you can continue to develop your skills.

- Focus: Once you have a good idea of which types of charts and patterns you like to use, concentrate on learning how to use them very well. Use a demonstration account with your Forex dealer to test out your charting skills for picking the best buy and sell points.

- Consistency: Be sure that you maintain your charts regularly. Preparing them daily even if you don't plan to trade that day will help you develop strong and consistent trading strategies. This daily routine will enable you to quickly recognize patterns and make good trading decisions.

The Least You Need to Know

- Learn to read and understand charts. They can give you a road map to the direction the currency market may be headed.

- Spotting trends will help you determine if the currency market is heading up or down.

- Recognizing patterns will help you spot possible breakouts and good trading opportunities.

Chapter 10

Exploring Fundamental Analysis

In This Chapter

- ◆ Flows of currency
- ◆ Policies and rates
- ◆ Economic red flags

Fundamental analysts look at the underlying economic conditions and use that information to attempt to predict a currency's current and future valuation. This is very different from technical analysts who believe all the information that is needed to predict the price of a currency and a directional trend is a database of historical prices.

It's important to understand both fundamental and technical analysis when making trading decisions. In this chapter, we focus on the key aspects of fundamental analysis that should be used by currency traders.

What Is Fundamental Analysis?

Fundamental analysts collect data about what is happening in the economy and try to understand how these economic conditions impact the current value of a particular currency, as well as predict what might happen to the currency's future value. Many things can impact the state of the economy, including monetary policy set by government agencies, capital and trade flows, production, and employment (or unemployment). Understanding these key economic indicators and how they impact the value of money is critical for currency traders.

Watching the Flows

Money flows in waves. Watching those flows can help you determine where your next best trading opportunity might occur. There are two types of money flows you need to watch—capital flows and trade flows. In Chapter 4, we discuss some key news sources for watching those flows.

Capital Flows

Capital flows gauge the amount of a currency that is bought or sold for the purpose of capital investment. When you read that a country has a positive capital flow balance, this means that foreign inflows of capital exceed the outflows of capital. The reverse is true if there is a negative flow balance.

There are two types of capital flows you need to watch—physical flows and portfolio flows. Physical flows involve investment activity that produces products and services, while portfolio flows involve the exchange of equities, such as stocks and bonds.

The physical flows currency traders want to watch include:

◆ Foreign direct investment—Whenever you read that a major corporation is building a plant in another country, it is considered a foreign direct investment. For example, if Coca-Cola builds a processing plant in China, that would be a foreign direct investment.

◆ Joint ventures—If you read about a U.S. corporation partnering with a corporation in another country, it is considered a joint venture. For example, if you read that Toyota and GM are working together to build a hybrid car, that would be a joint venture.

♦ Third-party licensing agreements—If you hear that a foreign company is buying the rights to patented products or business processes or the rights to use a brand name, this would fit in the category of third-party licensing agreements. For example, if you hear that Chinese computer makers have signed agreements to buy operating system software from Microsoft, that would be a third-party licensing agreement.

Any major deals affecting physical flows could move the currency market, because in order to carry out these agreements, currency would need to be bought and sold. Currently, most of the world's capital belongs to the United States, Europe, and Japan, while most of the world's cheapest labor is found in China, India, and other emerging nations.

What we see today in the business world is many agreements that send capital to the emerging nations through various means of physical flows. By doing this, they take advantage of cheap labor markets. In fact, the *World Bank* found that net private capital flows to developing countries in 2005 hit a record high of $491 billion, driven primarily by privatizations of formerly government-owned industries, mergers, and acquisitions.

Growth in the developing nations is also much stronger than that of the developed nations. China and India lead the pack. In 2005, China's economy grew by 9.9 percent and India's grew by 8 percent. Growth for the other emerging nations averaged 6.4 percent, while growth in the developed countries averaged 4.3 percent, down from 5.7 percent in 2004.

Money has been moving from developed to emerging nations for years, so why do we seem to

def•i•ni•tion

The **World Bank** provides financial and technical assistance to developing countries around the world. The bank is owned by 184 member countries and works to reduce global poverty and improve the living standards of people in developing countries. The bank provides low-interest loans, as well as interest-free credit and grants to developing countries for education, health, infrastructure, communications, and other purposes.

feel the economic pain in the United States more than we have in past years? One major factor that explains this new pain is the speed at which capital can flow. Today, massive amounts of capital can move quickly around the world through electronic transmission many times in a matter of seconds. In addition, the costs of moving this capital from one country to another dropped dramatically over the past 20 years, as barriers to currency trading were lifted (see Chapter 2 for more information about this change).

Unfortunately for U.S. workers, what all this means is that corporations that own all this capital have a wide variety of high-return investments for their money. As corporations find better investments outside the country, U.S. workers get downsized, yet U.S. corporation profits continue to rise dramatically.

Currency traders can make up for some of these lost wages by taking advantage of the money to be made as capital moves around the world. For example, when a U.S. corporation invests in a business in China, that company must sell dollars and buy Chinese yuan. The fact that many U.S. corporations are currently investing in China does not have a big impact on the value of the dollar because the Chinese yuan is pegged to the dollar, but that could change in the future if the yuan is allowed to flow freely. Generally when large amounts of a currency are sold, the currency will drop in value.

In addition to physical flows, you should also watch portfolio flows. These involve the buying and selling of stocks (equity market) and bonds (fixed-income market).

When a stock market rallies in any part of the world, this becomes an investment opportunity for investors in any other part of the world, thanks to the speed at which capital can flow. Geographic location is no longer a barrier for stock investors.

Why does this matter to currency traders? In order for investors to buy stocks in another country, they must first buy that country's currency. When a currency is in demand for stock investment, then the value of that currency will rise.

> ### Currency Corn
>
> Capital has flowed around the world since the days of Marco Polo, if not before. If you watched it move in Polo's time, you'd probably think you were watching a slow-motion movie. At first it moved very slowly as raw materials were traded, then it progressed to finished products. Next came financial capital, which moved slowly at first because barriers to trading currency were put in place by countries seeking to protect the value of their currency. Today those barriers are gone for the major currencies, allowing capital to flow much more quickly around the world, and increasing opportunities to make money in foreign currency trading.

If a stock market is headed into a free fall, people will want to get out of that market. That means that once they sell their stock in that country, they will also want to sell that country's currency, driving the value of the currency down as well. Major stock market moves can serve as either great opportunities to make money or as times of increased risk in foreign currency trading.

Some currency traders watch key global stock indexes to pick their trading opportunities, including:

- **Dow Jones Industrial Index (DOW)**—The DOW is the most widely used indicator of the overall condition of the stock market, but it only tracks 30 actively traded blue-chip stocks. The stocks tracked are picked by the editors of *The Wall Street Journal.* The DOW index was founded in 1896 by Charles Dow.

- **S&P 500**—The S&P 500 provides a broader picture of the U.S. stock market. It tracks a basket of 500 stocks, which actually reflects over 70 percent of the movement of the U.S. stock market. Companies are picked for the index based on their market size, liquidity, and industrial sector. The index was first created in 1957 by Standard & Poor's, primarily known for its credit-rating services.

- **Nasdaq Composite**—The Nasdaq Composite Index tracks primarily technology stocks, so it is not a good indicator of the broader stock market, but is a good indicator of what is happening in growth stocks. The index dates back to 1971, when the Nasdaq stock exchange was first created.

- **Nikkei Index**—The Nikkei index is the most respected index of Japanese stocks. The index is calculated using Japan's top 225 blue-chip companies on the Tokyo Stock Exchange. Many think of the Nikkei as the equivalent of the DOW index in the United States. It was even named the Nikkei Dow Jones Stock Average from 1975 to 1985. The index was started in 1950 by Japan's leading business newspaper, *The Nikkei*.

- **DAX 100**—The DAX 100 is an index of the 100 most heavily traded stocks in the German stock market.

- **FTSE 100**—This stock index tracks the top 100 stocks on the London Stock Exchange and is similar to the S&P 500. The index is co-owned by the *Financial Times* daily newspaper of London and the London Stock Exchange.

As a currency trader, if you see major movement in a stock market index, look for trading opportunities for the currencies impacted by the moves.

Fixed-income investments or bonds can also be attractive to investors because they offer more safety and a constant flow of income from the interest paid on them. In order to buy bonds in a foreign country, one must first buy the currency so bond purchases can also impact the value of a currency. Watch the yields on foreign bonds compared to U.S. bonds. When interest rates are higher outside the United States, you will see more investors buying foreign bonds, which means they likely are buying the currency with the most attractive bond interest rates and possibly selling U.S. dollars to do so.

Trade Flows

Another key indicator of where money is going can be seen in trade flows. The best indicator for watching trade flows is a country's net trade balance. Countries that are net trade exporters, meaning they export more goods and services than they import, will carry a net trade surplus. Countries with a net trade surplus are more likely to see their currencies rise in value.

Conversely, countries that have a trade deficit, meaning they import more goods and services then they export, could end up with a loss in the value of their currency. As the euro builds as an international currency, the value of the U.S. dollar could be more severely impacted by the United States' propensity to run huge trade deficits. When the U.S. government's rising debt levels are added to this, it could spell a recipe for disaster in the value of the U.S. dollar.

Capital Cautions

What will these rising trade deficits and debt levels mean for those of us who live in the United States? It will cost more for us to buy foreign goods and services as the value of the dollar weakens.

Monetary Policy and Interest Rates

Countries can dramatically alter economic activity within their borders by making changes to monetary policy. There are two key economic policy changes that most governments can control—interest rates and tax rates.

In the United States, interest rate policy is set by the U.S. Federal Reserve Bank (Fed), which is an independent entity under the aegis of the U.S. Congress. While the president appoints the Federal Reserve chairman, as well as the other members of the Fed's board of governors, he cannot control the decisions these appointees make. The Fed protects its independence fiercely, but it must report its activities periodically to Congress.

Through its reports to Congress and other key speeches, the Fed's chairman can quickly impact the global markets if he announces a major change in direction for the Fed's monetary policy. For example, if he announces an unexpected increase or decrease in interest rates, it will send shock waves through the stock market. Of course, that will in turn result in the buying and selling of currency, creating foreign currency trading opportunities.

A lowering of interest rates can initially stimulate a country's economic conditions, but if money flows too freely, inflation can set in. If a currency loses its value during an inflationary period, it will be punished in the currency markets.

An increase in interest rates tends to attract new capital flows and pushes up the value of a currency for at least the short term, but as other countries raise their interest rates, the benefit of the rate increase will be reduced.

Whenever a country's central bank changes interest rates, you can guarantee the markets will react. As you pick the currencies you plan to trade, don't forget to keep a close watch on any interest rate changes.

Major changes in tax policy can also impact the value of a country's currency. Generally, capitalists prefer tax cuts and reward a country that cuts taxes with an increase in its currency's value. But if those cuts create a major debt increase, it could result in a long-term loss of a currency's value as currency traders switch to safer countries where debt is not as high.

Economic Indicators

Economic indicators provide a snapshot of key parts of a country's economy. You can read stories almost every day about how well a country is doing based on some economic indicator. Popular indicators track employment, money supply, interest rates, housing starts, housing sales, production levels, purchasing statistics, consumer confidence, and many factors that impact the health of a country's economy.

While all these indicators are important, we're going to focus on just a few of the most critical ones. You could go crazy trying to keep your eye on all the indicators and what they mean. We've picked four key types of economic reports for you to watch—Gross Domestic Product (GDP), employment statistics, the Fed's Beige Book, and trade balance statistics.

Gross Domestic Product

The GDP is the total value of all final goods and services produced within a country's borders each year. This indicator measures the national income and output for a country.

Each quarter the government releases the percentage of growth in the GDP. Most industrial nations, such as the United States, Japan, and European countries, experience a GDP growth of between 3 and 5 percent. If growth falls below this level, it's usually a sign of trouble and an indication that the country's economy may be stalling or worse—heading into a recession. If growth climbs above that window, it could also be a sign of trouble—inflation. In extreme situations, the run-up could lead to a crash, like we saw during the late 1990s and early 2000s.

Developing countries can grow at a faster pace, but that too can lead to trouble. For example, China has been growing at a pace of 8 to 9 percent per year since 2003. However, too much growth and too much money can drive a country toward a severe economic downturn. When a country doesn't act quickly to stem its overheated growth, it can result in a crisis. Thailand experienced this with a major loss of its currency's value in the 1990s. Its crash led to currency speculation, failing banks, and falling stock prices. The Philippines, Indonesia, and Korea have faced similar problems.

If you want to find out if there are signs of trouble in a developing country, one good source of information is the World Bank, which regularly reports on economic indicators in the developing world. You can read its reports at www.worldbank.org.

Employment

Employment reports can be an important indicator of a country's economic health. When the economy is strong, jobs are created, but as the economy contracts, jobs are lost. If the economy is going too strongly and too many jobs are created, then wages begin to rise as companies compete for the best workers. Rising wages can lead to inflation, which will likely result in a country's central bank raising interest rates to cool the economy. People will then buy fewer goods as interest rates rise, which means less production is needed. When less production is needed, jobs get cut, leading to a weaker economy.

The country's central bank will stimulate the economy by lowering interest rates and starting the entire cycle yet again. Watching employment reports can help you determine where in this cycle a country's economy stands.

When the employment report is released, you should watch for three key factors—payroll, unemployment rate, and average hourly earnings growth.

- **Payroll.** This measures the change in the number of workers in a given month. In the United States, this report's estimates are based on a survey of larger businesses and government entities. It's important to compare this number to a monthly moving average for six or nine months to get a good idea of the trend for payrolls and employment. Expanding payrolls means the country's economy is growing. Contracting payrolls means the economy is heading for a slowdown.

- **Unemployment Rate.** This percentage measures the percentage of the civilian labor force actively looking for a job but not able to find one. This number can be skewed, especially during a weak economy—as workers get discouraged looking for work, they tend to drop off the unemployment lists. During particularly long periods of unemployment, the number of unemployed can be higher than shown in this rate.

- **Average Hourly Earnings Growth.** This number shows the growth rate of average hourly wages each month. This can be a good way to keep your eye on the potential for inflation. As wages increase, the possibility of inflation also increases.

Conversely, a high unemployment number can be good news and stimulate the economy. That's because high unemployment usually results in a lowering of interest rates, which can increase spending. When unemployment numbers improve and jobs are created, stock markets will likely fall because they are expecting the Fed to raise interest rates to slow things down again.

Beige Book

One of the easiest ways to get a good overview of what is happening throughout the U.S. economy is to read the Fed's Beige Book, which is officially known as the Summary of Commentary on Current Economic Conditions. This book is published eight times per year by the Federal Reserve Bank and includes anecdotal information on economic and business conditions in each of the Fed's districts.

Information for the book is collected by bank staff through interviews with key business leaders, economists, market experts, and other sources from within each of the bank's 12 districts. This book is like the Bible to the Federal Reserve Board of Governors. If the Beige Book shows warning signs of inflation, recession, or high unemployment, you are more likely to see the Fed act and change interest rates.

Wealth Builders

You can read the Beige Book online at the Fed's website. You can find a calendar for release dates of the book and links to each book at www.federalreserve.gov/FOMC/BeigeBook/2006/.
From this page, you can also research economic conditions and access Fed Beige Books dating back as far as 1970. If you want to find all the key economic indicators in one place, the Fed's Fred (Federal Reserve Economic Data) database is an excellent resource. You can access this online at research.stlouisfed.org/fred2.

Trade Balance

The most critical data you need to find out about the current and potential future status of a country's currency is its trade balance. Nations that regularly run a trade deficit can expect to see the value of their currency fall. The reason for this is that as a nation's currency flows overseas, it gets converted.

The two key indicators of trade balance to watch are balance of payments and balance of trade:

◆ Balance of payments measures the financial capital that flows from one nation to another. If more money flows in than out, a country has a positive balance of payments. Conversely, if more money flows out than in, a country has a negative balance of payments.

◆ Balance of trade calculates the sum of money in a specific country's economy by the selling exports minus the cost of buying imports. Transactions involving foreign investment in a country are also figured into this equation. A positive trade balance is called a trade surplus. A negative trade balance is called a trade deficit.

The more a nation's currency is sold rather than bought, the greater the risk that the demand for that currency will fall. When demand falls, prices drop. So far, the U.S. currency has not fallen dramatically, and that's primarily because capital investment in this country is still strong. This includes major real estate and business purchases by foreign companies and purchases of U.S. government debt by foreign entities (either governments or corporations). Also helping to keep the dollar propped up is the fact that many countries must have a supply of dollars to pay for oil from OPEC.

How long these two factors will keep the dollar afloat as trade deficits grow and debt levels increase is a big question. Eventually this market may fall.

How Should You Use Fundamental Analysis?

As a trader, you should make use of both fundamental and technical analysis. Technical analysis provides a map for analyzing a currency's price action and helps you recognize trends in those prices. Fundamental analysis helps you to determine what is actually happening in the market to explain the trends you see in your technical analysis. Using both types of analysis will help you make better trading decisions.

The Least You Need to Know

- Capital flows help you determine where the money is going and which currencies may be impacted by that movement.

- If you follow changes in monetary policy and interest rates, you will be able to recognize potential shifts in a currency's value.

- Economic indicators help you recognize economic trends, as well as the potential for a change in monetary policy.

Chapter **11**

Risks Faced When Trading Foreign Currency

In This Chapter

- ◆ Exploring the risks
- ◆ Borrowing money to trade
- ◆ Facing volatility
- ◆ Losing liquidity

Trading in foreign currency is risky business. Currency markets can be volatile, and it is highly speculative. You could lose the entire amount you deposited in your Forex account in a matter of minutes if the market moves against you.

You must understand the risks before you start trading. Many of the risks are similar to those you face in the stock market, but others are unique to foreign currency trading. In this chapter, we introduce you to the risks you may face when trading currency.

Leverage Risk

All currency traders use leverage to make a profit trading currency. Leverage is the use of borrowed money in an attempt to increase the potential return of a trade. Leverage is used in the currency markets because profits are made at exchange rate differences that are only fractions of a cent, so you must trade with large sums of money in order to make a notable profit.

Banks or brokers set the amount of leverage they will offer you. This is called "buying on margin." You won't find the strict government regulations regarding margin rules that you find in margin accounts available when trading stocks or options. We talk more about the rules for margin accounts in Chapter 13.

When a Forex dealer or broker approves your trading account, they set the rules for how much you can borrow—your margin allowance. Most Forex dealers allow you to trade on a 1 percent margin. That means with just $1,000 you can control $100,000 worth of currency. There are not many markets in which you will find that level of leverage, but remember increased leverage means you also have the potential to lose more money.

Capital Cautions

While trading hundreds of thousands of dollars may sound very exciting, remember that when you trade at these high volumes, even a minor mistake can wipe out all you have deposited in your account in a matter of minutes. Don't rush into trading your money. Read, take a course or two, and practice trading with a demonstration account before you start trading your hard-earned money. Never put more money at risk than you can afford to lose.

When you pick a pair of currencies you want to trade, the difference in the price at which you can buy and sell the currencies is just fractions of a cent. Each of these fractions is called a pip. For example, when you trade a standard lot in the currency pair EUR/USD (you can read more about currency pairs in Chapters 6 and 7), you can gain or lose $10 per pip. So if you buy five standard lots of 100,000 units (a total of 500,000), you could gain or lose $50 per pip.

When trading a lot size of 100,000 of any currency pair that is quoted out to 4 decimal places, the pip value will always be 10 units of the counter currency. If the counter currency is the same as the currency in which the account is funded, each pip will equal 10 units of the deposit currency. For example, for a trader with an account funded in U.S. dollars, one pip equals $10 on a 100,000 lot of EUR/USD. In cases where the counter currency is different than the currency the trader's account is funded in, each pip will still be worth 10 units, but it will have to be converted to the currency in which the account is funded to determine actual profit or loss amount.

If you are using 1 percent leverage and trade five lots, you would need to have $1,000 for each lot. Therefore, you would need $5,000 in your trading account.

Let's assume you bought five standard lots of this pair at the exchange rate of 1.2522 and it dropped by 100 pips to 1.2422 by the time you were able to sell it. Your loss would be $5,000—a complete wipeout.

Even a drop of just 10 pips, from 1.2522 to 1.2512, would be a loss of $500 or 10 percent of your money. Of course, using the same scenario, you stand to gain $5,000 if the currency moves in your direction with a 100 pip swing. We talk more about how to buy and sell currency in Chapter 13.

Market Risk

All traders, no matter what you are trading—currency, stock, options, or futures—face market risk. Market risk basically encompasses any price movement that impacts your trade unfavorably.

From the moment you first place your trade to the moment you successfully exit it, you are facing the risk that the price of the currency may move against your position. Of course, you're hoping that the market will move in your favor, but you can never be sure that it will.

When it comes to currency, there are two key factors that impact currency values—exchange rates and interest rates—so of course these both represent a type of risk for currency traders.

Exchange Rate Risk

Whenever you open a trade involving currency, whether you are trading through the Forex spot or forward market or using options or futures transactions, you face exchange rate risk. You are immediately exposed to the possibility that the exchange rate for the currency pair you've chosen will move against your position.

Exchange rates change every few seconds, so a loss due to exchange rate risk can happen very quickly. In just a few seconds, a profitable transaction can turn into a loss. We talk more about how to manage this loss potential using various trading tools in Chapters 12 and 13.

Currency Corn

Major global corporations manage their exchange rate risks in many different ways. Most seek to manage their exchange rate risk by buying options to hedge their bets against a change in exchange rates as they buy and sell raw materials or finished products around the world. About 5 percent of global corporations even speculate in currency trading. For example, Caterpillar turned losses in its core businesses into profits through its currency trading operations when the company was having a bad year in 1986. Its $100-million profit in foreign exchange trading turned its $24-million operating loss into a $76-million net profit.

Interest Rate Risk

The exchange rate is not the only thing that can impact the value of the currencies you hold. A change in interest rates by the central bank that manages the currency for the country can dramatically affect your currency positions involving the country whose rate was changed.

Wealth Builders

If you want to learn more about how corporations manage risks related to foreign currency exchange, read Gregory Millman's book, *The Floating Battlefield: Corporate Strategies in the Currency Wars*, published by Amacom in 1990.

For example, every time the Federal Reserve decides to raise or lower interest rates, the value of the U.S. dollar will be affected. Read more about the impact of interest rate changes in Chapter 5.

Generally, when a central bank announces an interest rate increase, the announcement will drive up the value of a currency because the higher rates increase demand for the currency. Conversely, a decrease in interest rates likely will result in selling of that currency, so it will likely drop in value due to the lower interest rate.

Counterparty Risk

When trading currency, you'll always face counterparty risk. Whenever you enter into a currency transaction, there must be two parties involved; one party is selling and the other party is buying. The person or entity with which you are trading is called the counterparty.

Whenever you trade with another party, you risk the possibility that the other party will not be able to meet his or her obligations. This is called counterparty risk.

You can avoid this risk by trading only with known entities with excellent credit ratings. You should investigate any entity that you intend to work with as a currency trader by researching whether any problems have been reported, such as insolvency or questions of ethical conduct. A good place to begin your research is the Commodity Futures Trading Commission (www.cftc.gov). We talk more about how to avoid currency fraud in Chapter 16.

Volatility Risk

Currency prices change every second, so you can see movement in a currency thousands of times per day. This makes currency trading a very volatile endeavor. Volatility is a key part of the currency trading experience, which can be an opportunity or a risk.

If volatility in a market scares you, you probably want to think about another way to make your money. There is absolutely no way to completely avoid volatility risk when you trade foreign currencies. The good news is that you can minimize your volatility risk by sticking to the major currency pairs involving the developed countries. We talk more about these pairs in Chapter 6.

Currency Corn
Many global corporations hire currency traders to manage their foreign exchange operations. With the large amounts of money they trade each year, they can earn hefty profits for the company by speculating and taking advantage of the volatility of the markets. For example, in 1992 there were many stories about how computer company Dell was speculating in foreign currency. Dell refused to comment on it, so financial analysts scoured its financial statements to figure out whether or not this was true. No one succeeded in proving it one way or another until one of Dell's foreign exchange traders was looking for a job and the press found out he had indicated on his resumé that he had traded $1 billion in currency contracts.

Liquidity Risk

You won't likely face liquidity risk when trading any of the major currency pairs. Over $1.9 trillion are traded daily, so you're not likely to find it difficult to get rid of a currency when you want to.

But (of course there's a but), if you do decide to take on more risk by trading emerging countries' currencies, liquidity risk can be a factor. Liquidity risk means that you might not be able to sell a currency you hold when you want to sell it. Of course, that is not likely to happen with the U.S. dollar, the yen, or the euro (or any other major currency), but you could have a hard time finding a buyer if you hold the currency of an emerging country. Liquidity can be particularly tricky if the country whose currency you hold just experienced a major change in political leadership—whether a violent coup or an unexpected election result.

Country Risk

When trading currency, what is happening in a particular country could greatly impact the value of its currency. There are a number of different types of country risks—political risk, regulation risk, legal risk, and holiday risk.

Currency Corn

Some companies must operate regularly in countries that face hyper-inflation or during a period of war. Managing foreign exchange trading can be crucial to their ability to operate profitably in these difficult environments. For example, in the 1980s and 1990s, Union Carbide Corporation had a task force of 30 people who managed currency operations throughout the corporation. Operating units sold their foreign currency exposures to this currency risk management unit. Dow Chemical bought Union Carbide in 2001 and the currency risk management is done through the parent company.

Political Risk

Political risk involves the stability of the country's government. As long as you stick to trading currency from countries whose governments are relatively stable, you won't face severe problems with political risk. Even if a developed country faces a major change in political leaders, it's not likely the currency will face a dramatic shift in price, but you will likely see some price movement depending upon the new leader's economic policies and the expected impact of the new leader on the country's economy.

When emerging countries face major political turmoil, you will most likely see a drop in the value of that country's currency as people try to sell it in order to get out before an even bigger fall. If you are trading the currency of an emerging country that does not have a large volume of sales even before the change in political leadership, you likely will face not only the political risk, but also liquidity risk as you try to sell.

For example, Mexico's closely fought presidential race in 2006 could have driven the value of the peso down dramatically if the leftist party leader had won the race. Instead, Mexico's currency surged after Felipe Calderon won because he pledged to continue the economic policies of Vicente Fox, which the capital markets have supported.

Currency Corn

Operating in a war zone can be particularly difficult for a company. Halliburton has been doing just that as it supports the U.S. military in its operations overseas. In its 2002 annual report, Halliburton stated that it does not trade currency for speculation, but does for operations. It also talks about the difficulty of working with nontraded currencies. When operating in a country where currency cannot be traded, Halliburton states that it prices its products and services in these countries to attempt to cover the cost of exchange rate devaluations. Halliburton reported that it historically incurred transaction losses in its nontraded currencies.

Regulation Risk

If a government changes regulations that impact a country's currency, you face the potential of a loss because of regulation risk. Sometimes, especially when you are trading currencies involving emerging countries, the central bank will change a regulation that makes it more difficult for you to trade that currency.

For example, if you are a foreigner who holds currency in a country that changes its regulations to make it more difficult for you to hold the currency of that country, you may be forced into a position of selling the currency no matter what the loss may be to you. If you do decide to trade currencies of emerging countries, be sure you carefully research its current and potential future regulations.

You are not likely to face regulation risk in currencies of major developed nations. These currencies have been trading unimpeded on the spot market for years and are not likely to be impacted by changes in regulations.

You can read more about emerging countries and their fixed-float systems that could face regulatory change in Chapter 7.

Legal Risk

You face legal risks whenever you do business outside the country in which you live. When currency trading is involved, you often trade with a counterparty that does not reside in the same country as you do. If the counterparty were to default on the deal, you could face a legal risk depending upon which country has jurisdiction over the contract. How the contract can be enforced will depend on that jurisdiction.

If the host country of the counterparty enforces contract law differently than your home country, you could find it difficult to resolve the question. In fact, the host country could even determine that your contract was invalid or illegal. You can lose your entire position in that host country's currency.

Be sure you know who you are buying from and under which country's law the contract will be mediated if there is a problem. If you find out that U.S. contract law will not be the prevailing law, be certain you understand the law of the country that will prevail if there are any problems before you get involved in the deal.

As long as you work with a retail broker or dealer who is registered and regulated by the National Futures Association or the Commodity Futures Trading Commission, you likely will never have to worry about legal risk. But if you decide to trade with a broker or dealer not based in the United States or not regulated by the NFA or CFTC, this risk could become a big problem if you have trouble enforcing a contract.

Holiday Risk

Each country celebrates different holidays on different days. Holiday risk involves the possibility that the currency you wish to trade cannot be traded because of a bank holiday in that country. Different religious, political, or government holidays can stop the trading in the currency if the banks are closed. That could mean you can't get your money when you want it, and you will have to wait for the banks to reopen after the holiday.

When trading foreign currency, be sure you know the key holiday celebrations when the banks will be closed and plan your trading around these holidays.

Avoid Risks by Trading Through Regulated Entities

While there is no way to totally eliminate your exposure to risk, you can avoid some of these risks by being certain that you trade solely through regulated entities.

If you do business with a nonbanking institution not regulated by a government entity, you are operating in unprotected waters. You will have no regulatory agency to turn to for help if you face a problem. If you work with unregulated firms, you will be operating under the rule of *caveat emptor*, which is Latin for "let the buyer beware."

If you do plan to work with a non-U.S. entity, be sure to research the organization through the Bank for International Settlement (www.bis.org) before depositing any money with the entity. The BIS has the responsibility of evaluating foreign exchange trading institutions on a global basis. Unfortunately you can't look up the information online; you must call or write BIS to research a foreign entity.

Some clearinghouses have paved the way to help you avoid counter-party risk and other risk associated with foreign exchange trading. Be sure to use all resources available to you to minimize foreign exchange trading risks—it's risky enough without them.

The Least You Need to Know

- The greatest risk all traders face is leverage risk. No matter what currency you trade, you must borrow significantly in order to make money because profits are made on differences of fractions of a cent.

- Foreign exchange traders face numerous risks inherent to the process of trading money globally. Become familiar with these risks and how you can minimize your exposure.

- Trading currencies of emerging nations exposes you to a number of risks you are not likely to face if you stick to trading the major currencies of developed industrialized nations. These risks include liquidity risks, political risks, regulation risks, and legal risks.

Part **4**

Tools for Trading

In this part, we move on to developing your money strategies and talk about how you can place orders. We also introduce you to mini accounts that help you start small and explain how you can get involved in the Forex market with professional money managers. Finally, we talk about how to avoid money fraud.

Chapter 12

Developing Your Money Strategies

In This Chapter

- ◆ Managing your money
- ◆ Disciplining yourself
- ◆ Controlling your emotions
- ◆ Minimizing your risks

We're sure you've heard stories of people making millions of dollars trading Forex in a matter of hours or even minutes. While that may have happened for a lucky few, more often than not you won't be seeing that kind of win. You could even lose more than the total balance in your Forex account in a matter of minutes if you're not careful.

In this chapter, we talk about how to manage your money and how to develop a disciplined trading plan. We also discuss the importance of keeping your emotions in check, as well as risk-management strategies.

Developing a Money-Management Plan

When you decide to trade Forex, you're trading with the big boys—central banks, international financial institutions, and major corporations. You also need to think big and understand where trading Forex fits with your portfolio-management strategies. First, ask yourself these three questions:

◆ Do I understand the foreign exchange market fully, as well as the risks I'll be taking?

◆ Does trading Forex fit with my long-term portfolio-management strategies?

◆ Can I spend the time needed to research this market daily and make sound Forex trading decisions?

If your answer is "no" to any of these questions, you're not ready to trade Forex.

That said, if you can answer "yes," then think of Forex money management as you would if you were managing any other business.

◆ **Develop a business plan.** Determine how much money you want to risk, what return you expect to make, and how much time you will be able to devote to the business. We recommend that you start trading with no more than about 2 percent of your portfolio assets. When you are confident that you know what you are doing, you can increase that to 5 percent. You probably would not want to put more than 5 percent of your portfolio assets in such a risky business venture. As you decide on your return expectations, remember that even the best money managers aim for a goal of 15 to 20 percent annual return over the long term.

Capital Cautions

Never put more than 5 percent of your portfolio at risk for Forex trading. Remember that this is a highly volatile market and you could lose all the money in your Forex account in a matter of minutes if the market turns dramatically against you.

◆ **Set up your business office.** You should determine what physical assets your business will have, including your workspace and computer equipment. The more structured you make your business surroundings, the greater control you will have over your business activities. Don't set up your business periodically on your dining room table. If that's all you can afford to do, you're not ready for serious trading. You will need a quiet space where you can research your trades and develop your charts.

♦ **View your holdings as inventory.** The currency pairs you hold should be treated like inventory, something you plan to buy and sell. Don't get emotionally tied to your inventory.

♦ **Accept your mistakes.** Every business person makes mistakes as they are building a business. That's true for Forex traders as well. Don't try to defend a trading mistake. Take your loss and move on. If your choice no longer makes good business sense, make that cold, hard decision to exit the position before a small loss turns into a big one—which can happen in seconds when market conditions are volatile.

♦ **Take your profits.** When you have a healthy profit and reach your exit point, don't hold on to the inventory. No one can accurately pick the top or bottom of any trade every time. Don't push your luck; follow your business plan.

♦ **Stick to your trading plan.** Once you pick a trading strategy, stick with your plan. Don't change it in the middle of the trade if things go sour. Follow your plan and then assess your mistake so you won't make it again. Many traders learn more from their mistakes than their successes.

A business in Forex trading is a 24-hour business. Dramatic moves can occur at any time, depending on world conditions. For example, when Hezbollah and Hamas both struck Israeli territory within days of each other in July 2006, a war erupted. No one expected the moves nor did they know the moves would develop into a war in the Middle East. Oil prices skyrocketed and the money markets became more volatile within hours of the start of the war.

Capital Cautions

Unexpected storms or earthquakes can also dramatically impact the money markets quickly. If you are trading currency in a region that was hit, be sure to carefully watch what happens to each of your currency pairs.

Taking Steps to Discipline Your Trades

Every Forex trader needs to develop a sound trading strategy that they can follow regularly. We won't recommend a specific strategy. That's something you need to develop for yourself based on your own emotional tendencies, as well as your knowledge and understanding of the marketplace.

But no matter what strategies you develop, you should use the classic approach to trading Forex—the inverted pyramid approach. This approach uses both fundamental (Chapter 10) and technical (Chapter 9) analysis to help you develop your trading plan.

Classic trading model—the inverted pyramid.

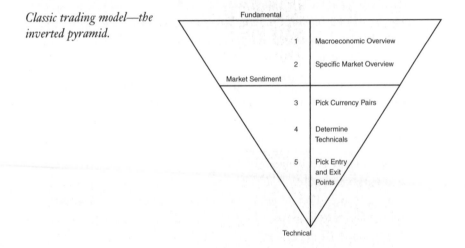

Here are the 5 steps to developing your trading plan:

Step 1: Take a macroeconomic view. Start your research by looking at the economic conditions around the world. What are the key pressures driving economic forces—including wars, oil prices, trade agreements among nations, storms, earthquakes, or holiday shopping? Look at whether the economy is being viewed globally in a generally pessimistic (most people expect things to get worse) or optimistic (most people expect things to get better) way. One of the easiest ways to judge this quickly is to watch one of the business cable news networks. We talk about good news sources in Chapter 4.

Step 2: Find news about specific money market conditions. Start focusing on what is happening in the money markets. If something could dramatically affect the money markets, all the business analysts will be talking about it. For example, if there is going to be a major rate meeting by one of the key central banks, such as the Federal Reserve in the United States or the Bank of England, we can guarantee there will be much speculation about what the central bank might do regarding a possible rate increase or decrease.

Once you've completed Steps 1 and 2, you should have a good idea of what the *market sentiment* is around the world, as well as in the countries on which you plan to focus your attention.

def•i•ni•tion

Market sentiment reflects the general mood surrounding the currency market. Understanding this general mood will help you develop a plan based on the expected behavior of the market, which can be critical to developing a good trading plan.

Economic indicators include any variable that gives you an idea of where the market may be headed, such as new employment statistics or trading balances.

Step 3: Pick your currency pairs. Once you have a good understanding of the currency market, you will be able to pick the currency pairs you wish to trade. You want to focus on pairs that may be volatile that day, week, or month—whatever your trading horizon might be. Decide which *economic indicators* will be the most important for market moves during the window of your trading plan. Also look at the recent trends in prices for the currency pairs you're considering trading. Do you see a strong trend or do you see a lot of volatility (no clear direction)? Use this step to narrow down the potential currency pairs for which you expect to set up a trading plan.

Step 4: Determine your basic technical points. Start using your favorite chart types to look for signs of support (a point on your chart at which sellers won't let the price fall below as they start buying the currency pair) and resistance (a point on the chart at which buyers won't let the price go above as they stop buying the currency pair). Use this information to pick currency pairs you want to trade based on the direction in which you expect the market to move. The fundamental information you gathered in Step 2 will help confirm the trends you are seeing in your charts.

Step 5: Pick your entry and exit points. Fine-tune your trading plan by actually picking your entry and exit points. If you look at the charts and still don't know how to do that, you need to spend more time learning how to apply technical analysis. As you become more comfortable with it, you'll pick the tools that best match your trading style and your knowledge or abilities. You must know both your entry and exit points before you even try to make the trade. Determine your plan and stick to it!

As you are learning how to use the inverted pyramid method, test your successes or failures with the method by opening a demonstration account with a Forex broker. We discuss how to choose a broker in Chapter 13. We also talk about trading platforms in Chapter 8. Practice trading with your plan and see if it works before using your hard-earned cash for a live account.

Getting Your Emotions in Check

When trading, your emotions can jump up and down almost as quickly as the market. While you can't deny your emotions, the key is to keep them under control so you can stick to your plan. But some people don't have the emotional stamina to even try to trade.

Ask yourself these questions:

♦ Does the idea of losing money keep you up at night?

♦ Can you not read the financial news without reacting emotionally?

♦ Do you make trading decisions quickly based on the latest tip you've heard?

If you answered "yes" to these questions, you probably don't have the emotional make-up to be a successful Forex trader. Forex traders must remain calm and focused on their plans. They must research the currency pairs they watch regularly. It is best if you can set aside time to watch the market daily, even if you don't plan to trade daily. By paying close attention to moves in the markets on a daily, consistent basis, you will be able to understand when there is a long-term trend driving the market or when the market takes a different direction.

One of the hardest things for some traders to do is to sell a position they are attached to. Don't get too attached. Remember that it is a business. You write a business plan (trading plan) and you follow that plan. Don't let your emotions take control and get you to alter your plans.

We know that can be easier said than done. You spend days, weeks, or months researching the markets and finally develop a strategy and plan that works for you.

If your plan works brilliantly, you have a sizeable profit. Now it's time to sell or buy according to your plan. But you just can't break away. You may want to ride the trade to the top, but don't. The fall can be quick and you could lose all you gained. Don't let your emotions drive your trading decisions; let your plan be your guide.

Emotions can also make it hard for you to sell, even if the exit point you set to minimize a loss is approaching quickly. You just can't figure out how you were so wrong and don't want to admit to a mistake. You still think it's a good trade and you want to hold on just a bit longer to try to prove yourself right. Don't do it. Letting go can be hard to do, but keep yourself focused on your plan and don't let your emotions take control.

Most Forex brokers offer commission-free trades. It's not like trading stock, where you must worry about the costs of getting in and out of a position. Get out, take your profits, or accept your losses. It doesn't cost you anything to re-enter the trade if you decide that's what you want to do.

Then take a deep breath. Take another look at your plan and determine whether you still think it's a good one and if you might consider different points for entering and exiting a new trade that reflects the recent market moves.

Do a calm, focused job of researching your position again. If a position moved much differently than you expected, do more research to see what might be different in both fundamental and technical analysis assumptions. It could be that a major economic shock that you missed took control of the markets after you set your plan.

Try to find the reason for the difference from your expectations. Even if you aren't going to trade that pair again in the next day, week, or month, understand why you made a mistake so you don't repeat your mistake again in the future.

Risk-Management Strategies

The best way to manage your risk is by setting up orders to take your profits when you first open your position. That way you don't risk getting caught up emotionally in the winning moment and ride your profits to a loss.

Set up stop-loss orders when you first open your position. That way your logic will be in control rather than your greed or emotional disappointment if the trade doesn't go as planned.

We talk about how to place orders in Chapter 13, but in this chapter, we want to explore how you can use limit orders (take profit) and stop-loss orders (minimize loss) to help you manage your risk.

Limit Orders (Take Profit)

Use a limit order to protect your profits. This will get you set up to exit the Forex market as planned without letting your emotions get the better of you. Avoid being tempted to ride a gain that could turn into a loss by sticking with the trade for too long.

If you are shorting a currency pair (selling), your broker's system should allow you to place a limit order below the current market price. When selling a currency pair, the profit zone is below the current price. The opposite is true if you are going long (buying) on a currency pair.

The system will allow you to set up a limit order to secure your profits at a price above the current market price. When buying a currency pair, the profit zone is above the current price. The take-profit order helps you maintain a disciplined trading strategy.

Don't set it up or change your limit order after watching your order for a while without carefully reviewing and updating your fundamental and technical analysis. Set up the limit order at the same time as you make your trade.

Since you don't pay commissions, you can always develop a new plan to buy or sell the same pair again, so it's better not to get into the practice of changing your limit or stop/loss orders. Instead, let them play out and develop a new plan for the next trade based on the information learned during your previous trades.

Stop-Loss Orders (Minimize Loss)

Use stop-loss orders to minimize your losses. Set up your stop-loss order at the time of your trade to protect yourself from being driven by your emotions. A stop-loss order lets you set up an exit point as you enter a trade that will get you out of your trade before your losses become too large.

If you short a currency pair, the stop-loss order should be set above the current price. Remember that when you are shorting a pair, the profit zone is below the price of the pair. If you go long on a currency pair, set up your stop-loss order below the current market price.

Obviously, you hope your stop-loss orders will never be needed, but don't forget to set them. When they are needed, you want the logic you used to set your entry and exit prices as you developed your plan to be in control, not your emotions.

Picking the Right Points

You're probably wondering how to determine where to set your limit and stop-loss orders. Many traders set their stop-loss orders closer to their opening price than their limit orders.

For example, a guideline you can follow when you're getting started is to set your stop-loss point at 30 pips and your take-profit orders at 100 pips.

Where you set your stop-loss and limit orders is purely up to you. The tighter the point, the less risky your trade will be, but remember if you set your order points too tight, normal market volatility could trigger your order long before you want it to do so. To make money you have to move outside the normal volatility range, so you do have to take some risk.

Another general rule most traders follow is to go long or neutral when you see a bull market. Go short or neutral if you believe the market conditions are ripe for a bear market.

Don't trade against the bull or bear trend. You will suffer emotional distress and will most likely suffer losses as well.

The Least You Need to Know

- ◆ Think of Forex trading as a business. Develop a business plan, set up your workspace, and think of your currency holdings as inventory that should be bought and sold.

- ◆ Discipline your trading strategies by using the inverted pyramid method.

- ◆ Control your emotions. Let your logic rather than your emotions determine your entry and exit points for a trade.

- ◆ Use stop-loss and limit orders and stick by them to ensure that your logic rather than your emotions dictate your trades.

Chapter 13

How to Place Orders

In This Chapter

- ◆ Terms for trading
- ◆ Borrowing to trade
- ◆ Picking a broker or dealer
- ◆ Ordering currency
- ◆ Calculating profits and losses

As a Forex trader, you'll be placing orders either to buy or sell currency. The basic process is not difficult, but you do need to understand certain terms unique to trading.

In this chapter, we review the trading terms for placing an order, explain the process of borrowing money to buy money, sort out how to pick your broker or dealer, review the basics of placing an order, and explore the types of orders.

Reviewing Key Trading Terms

If you've traded stocks, you'll find many of the terms for trading Forex to be similar, but with a slightly different twist. This section covers some key terms you should be sure you understand before placing an order.

Long/Short

When you first enter the Forex market you either go long by buying a currency or go short by selling a currency. When a currency is going up, you want to buy that currency so you go long. For example, if after researching currencies you learn that euros are expected to increase in value relative to the U.S. dollar, you would buy euros and sell U.S. dollars.

The opposite is true if your research shows that a currency is expected to decrease in relative value. Then you would short the currency by selling it and buying one that is expected to rise.

Positions

A position is an open trade. Every time you take a position in the Forex market, it involves someone buying and selling each currency in the pair while someone else has to be willing to sell and buy the corresponding currencies.

You should have no trouble trading a currency pair as long as there is liquidity in the market for that pair. If you are trading the major currencies, you should be able to find a willing buyer or seller, called a counterparty.

You will usually close out a position with your broker by reversing the original transaction. For example, if you bought Japanese yen with U.S. dollars, you would close the trade by selling Japanese yen for U.S. dollars.

Bid/Offer

When you see a quote for a currency pair, you will actually see two prices. One is the price at which the Forex broker or dealer is willing to sell the currency, which is called the offer or the ask. The other is the price at which the Forex market maker is willing to buy the currency, which is called the bid. This can also be viewed in terms of the trader, where the bid is the price at which a customer can sell, and the offer is the price at which a customer can buy. The bid price is always lower than the offer price, and is listed as the first price in a quote.

Spread

The spread is the difference in pips between the bid and the ask price for a currency. Forex brokers and dealers make money from the spread rather than with commissions, so you may notice a difference in the size of the spreads offered by different brokers, dealers, and banks.

Most brokers and dealers advertise that you can trade Forex commission-free because they make their money on the spread. Be sure you understand how the broker or dealer is being compensated before opening an account. Most spreads result in a cost of $10 to $40 per trade. Some Forex brokers hide additional fees in a wide spread, so review the spread carefully with your broker and be sure you understand your trading costs.

Wealth Builders

Always look for a broker or dealer who consistently offers tight spreads (which means the bid and ask are close in price)—especially on the major currency pairs. It will save you money.

Exchange Rate

Exchange rates are given in terms of the base currency and pricing (or terms) currency. The base currency is always shown first in a currency pair. If you are buying the base currency, the exchange rate is the amount you would pay or receive depending on the value of the base currency in terms of the pricing currency. Conversely, if you are selling the base currency, the exchange rate is how much you'll pay or receive for one unit of that currency.

For example, if the pair is shown as USD/JPY, the U.S. dollar is the base currency and the Japanese yen is the terms currency. So a quote of USD/JPY to sell USD for JPY at a price of 114.72 would mean for each U.S. dollar you could get 114.72 Japanese yen.

In Forex trading, the exchange rate will always be given as a pair when you are buying or selling because you are always selling one currency to buy another.

Pip

A pip is the pricing unit used in Forex trading. A pip is the smallest change in price that can be made in a currency. It is one unit of price change in the bid/ask price of a currency and is denoted by the last number behind the decimal point of the price. For example, if you receive a quote for the pair USD/JPY (U.S. dollar/Japanese yen) of 114.78/114.81, the spread is 3 pips.

Bull/Bear

When a market is described as a bull market, the general market is moving upward. If the bears are in control of a market, then the general market is moving downward.

Leverage

If you want to make money trading Forex, you'll most likely need to borrow money because the price differences in currency, which are what you will make your profit or loss on, are only fractions of a cent. When you borrow money to trade, it is called leverage.

Leverage is the amount of money a Forex broker or dealer will lend you for your trading activities. A common leverage option is 100 to 1. That means for every unit you use of your own capital, the broker will lend you 100 units. So for an account with $5,000, you can trade up to $500,000 of currency.

Capital Cautions

Margin accounts can make you responsible for losses that exceed the dollar amount you put into the account. Don't trade on margin unless you understand how much money you are putting at risk. Be prepared to accept losses that can exceed the amount of money you put into a margin account. While some brokers or dealers have policies in place to take you out of the market before you reach a negative balance, it cannot always be avoided during market gaps.

While it might sound exciting that you can trade half a million dollars for just $5,000, remember that while leverage does help you maximize your profits, it also increases your risk for substantial losses. When you're first getting started in Forex, it's a good idea to start much smaller.

To avoid taking on too much risk and to be sure you'll have enough money to cover any losses, it's a good idea to limit each trade to just 5 or 10 percent of your useable margin. That way if you do take a sizeable loss, you'll have enough in your account to cover that loss without having to dig deeper into your pockets.

Watch your useable margin as you trade. As you build your account, you'll be able to buy more lots, but if you take it slowly and follow the basic rule of not putting more than 5 to 10 percent of your useable margin in one basket, you'll minimize your risk. This will allow you to diversify your currency pairs and keep better control on your loss potential. You may also have a better chance of building your account with steady profits.

If your useable funds go into the negative, you will get a margin call. This means that if you don't come up with the money required to maintain your account quickly, the positions you hold will be sold to cover your losses.

Most Forex dealers will give their clients between two and five days to cover a margin call. If you cannot bring your account up to the specified minimum, your broker or dealer has the right to sell your positions to cover your account balance. A margin call is not a bad thing—its purpose is to protect you and your capital. Be sure you read the fine print on your margin account contract. Also, discuss with your dealer how margin calls are handled and how much time you'll have to answer a call.

Wealth Builders

Be patient as you build your Forex account and don't put too much of your money into one currency pair. Follow the rule of trading no more than 5 to 10 percent of your useable margin on one transaction. You can minimize your risk and work toward steadily building your profits.

When your useable margin drops too low (that level will be set by your broker when you open an account), you won't be able to trade on your current positions. You'll get a message on your screen such as "account in untradeable condition." You'll probably need to put more money into your account in order to trade.

> **Capital Cautions**
>
> You can lose your entire account balance if you're not careful, but you aren't likely to lose your house on a margin call. By putting on the brakes when your useable margin falls below a certain point, a good broker is actually protecting you from a more significant loss. Although you may initially get angry when you can't trade, it's a good thing and for your own protection.

Many Forex dealers no longer use a margin call system because the market moves too fast for traders to respond. All money could be lost too quickly. Instead, dealers set a minimum margin percent requirement, such as 25 percent of the account equity. If the account falls below that percentage, all holdings are liquidated. This protects the trader from losing everything. That way the trader will have enough money left after liquidation to begin trading again.

Choosing a Broker or Dealer

When you start looking for a company to open an account with, you'll find there are hundreds of websites promising quick riches. Most will promise you commission-free trades, but watch out for the hidden costs and those that are not so hidden.

Remember that the way most brokers or dealers make money is based on the spread between the bid and ask price. Always look for tight spreads to save money.

But more importantly, you need to find an established and reputable dealer. Forex dealers have relationships with large banks or financial institutions because of the large sums of capital that are involved.

Your best bet is to work with a dealer that has Futures Commission Merchant (FCM) status and can cut the middleman out of the equation. Co-author Gary Tilkin's company, GFT, provides this type of service. Dealers can save you fees that you may pay with a broker.

If you do decide to work with a broker, be sure you find one that is affiliated with an FCM. An FCM can handle futures contract orders and can extend credit to customers. If based in the United States, your broker should also be registered with the Commodity Futures Trading Commission (CFTC) and can be a member of the National Futures Association (NFA).

Wealth Builders

In rare cases, there are some brokers that are not regulated at all. Stay away from them. Any person can advertise himself as a Forex broker without becoming registered with the regulatory agencies, so do your homework. Make sure that your broker has gone through the hoops to become registered. You can find out very quickly by using the National Futures Association's Background Affiliation Status Information Center at www.nfa.futures.org/basicnet.

In Chapter 8, we discuss trading platforms and some of the top online dealers that provide services to individual Forex traders.

Exploring Order Types

You can use several different types of orders to trade Forex. We're going to introduce you to the five key types—market orders, limit orders, stop orders, stop-limit orders, and order cancels order.

Market Order

A market order is the simplest and most basic order you can place. You see a trade you want and place an order to make the trade.

The problem with a market order is that you are not always guaranteed that the actual trade your broker completes will match the precise entry point that you saw on your screen. If you are trying to guarantee a particular price on execution, a market order is not a good selection.

The Forex market moves so fast that by the time your trade is executed, even if it is less than a second later, the price of the currency pair could change. The quotes you see on your screen may not be accurate because the market may have moved so fast that the price you saw no longer exists.

Limit Order

A better type of order to place when buying or selling a currency is called a limit order. This type of order allows you to specify the price at which you want to buy or sell the currency pair.

If you are looking to buy a currency, you would place a limit order specifying that you will buy the currency at a specific price or lower. That way you won't end up paying more for the currency than what you specified as the appropriate entry point.

If you are looking to sell a currency, you would place a limit order specifying that you will sell the currency at a specific price or higher. That way you won't end up with less than the price that you chose as the appropriate exit point.

Wealth Builders

Some brokers may charge more for a limit order than a market order, but this is not a place where you should be thrifty. In this type of fast-moving market, you want the extra protection of a limit order.
If your broker charges too much for limit orders, find another broker, but don't cut corners by placing market orders. Most dealers, including GFT, offer limit orders at no additional charge.

There are two types of limit orders you can place—good til canceled and good for the day.

- Good til Canceled (GTC) orders remain in play until you decide to cancel the order. You have the responsibility to monitor your outstanding orders, so pay close attention to your standing limit orders to be sure you do still want them to be executed.

- Good for the Day (GFD) orders remain in play through the day and are automatically removed by your broker at the end of the day. Because the Forex market has the advantage of being a 24-hour market, a variation of GFD in Forex is "Good until close of." With this added twist you indicate which currency pair you want to indicate as GFD and what geographical market you want it to correspond to. For example, you might want your EUR/USD order to be canceled when the London market closes.

Stop Order

When you place a stop order, you set in place an order that will automatically be executed when your price is hit. When the price is hit, the order becomes a market order and will be executed as soon as possible.

Stop orders are used by traders to lock in profits or limit losses. For example, suppose you decided that you wanted to trade the currency pair USD/JPY. After researching your numbers, you saw that the best entry point was 116. You placed a limit order and purchased the yen for 116.

You expect the yen to gain in relative value and you want to liquidate your position when it hits 112. You see that the yen moves to a price of 114. You've picked the right direction for the currency and want to lock in your profits. You would then place a stop order at 114.5, just in case the yen starts moving in the other direction, to protect your profit. If the yen does end up losing value and heads back up to 116, your broker would automatically execute the stop order and protect your profits between 116 and 114.5.

If the currency is very volatile and moving up and down between 116 and 112, your stop order could be executed too soon. The market might make it down to your target exit point of 112, but after your stop is already executed.

Also, your stop order is not a guaranteed exit price. When the stop price is hit, it becomes a market order and will be executed at the best possible price as quickly as possible. So if the market is moving rapidly, you could end up with an order executed at a price significantly different than the price you specified in your stop order.

Stop-Limit Order

Your best bet if you want to guarantee a price is to place an order that uses the benefits of both a stop order and a limit order, called a stop-limit order. If you place a stop order, but are worried that the market may move too quickly for the order to be executed in time, then you can include a limit order as part of the stop order.

When you use a stop-limit order, the stop becomes a limit order rather than a market order and won't be executed unless your broker can get the price you specified or better.

Remember, a limit order does prevent the trade from being executed. If the market is moving so fast that your broker or dealer doesn't have enough time to execute the order at the price you specified, you could end up missing the opportunity for your order to be executed completely.

Order Cancels Order

Sometimes you'll want to use a more complicated order that actually allows you to place two limit or two stop orders at the same time. You can actually place one order to buy a currency at a specific price and one order to sell the same currency at a specific price.

For example, suppose you see the pair USD/JPY at a price of 116. In researching the currency, you saw some data indicating that there may be a breakout increasing the value of the yen to 117 and other data indicating that the yen may drop in value to 115. In this case, you might place a buy limit order at 115.5 and a sell limit order at 116.5. If the market moves toward 117, the sell limit order would be executed and the buy limit ordered would be canceled.

Trailing Stop Order

With a trailing stop order, you can set your stop order to continue to follow the price movement (in real time) by specifying the distance, in pips, you would like your stop to move—depending on the market direction and type of stop order placed.

For example, you have an open position where you bought (went long) one lot (100,000 units) of USD/JPY at 108.50. You are expecting the pair to move 50 pips to 109 but want to limit your loss should volatile market conditions move against you. You could set up an automatic trailing stop to exit your position at 108.70 (thus automatically stopping a loss).

Placing Trades—GFT's DealBook® 360 Example

We're sure you've realized by now that placing a Forex order requires you to understand a lot about the currency you trade, as well as the type of order you want to place. The actual process of placing an order is pretty simple, but do pay close attention to the details.

You usually can't call your dealer and say you made a mistake. By the time you do, the price will have changed numerous times and your order likely can't be reversed. This can be even worse if you are dealing with a broker who is not a primary market-maker.

Now we'll take you through the steps of actually placing an order using GFT's DealBook® 360.

Step 1: Pick the currency pair you want to trade. After clicking on New Order, your first step is to pick the currency pair you want to trade. In the following figure, we show you how you click on the arrow next to the symbol box and a drop-down menu will give you the currency options. In this example, we scrolled down the list to USD/ JPY.

Capital Cautions

The quickest way to lose money when trading Forex is to make a mistake when you place your orders. Every type of ordering system for Forex provides some way to confirm your order. Don't quickly click "Yes" at the bottom of the screen; read your orders carefully before confirming them.

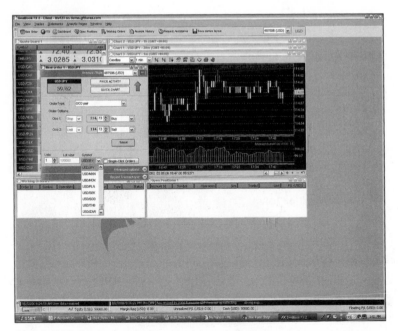

Step 1: Pick the currency pair you want to trade.

Step 2: Pick the order type you want to place. Next you want to pick the type of order that you want to place. To do this, click on the arrow next to order type and you'll get a drop-down menu. In the following figure, we show you the drop-down order menu that includes market order, limit order, and OCO (order cancels order). In this example, we picked OCO.

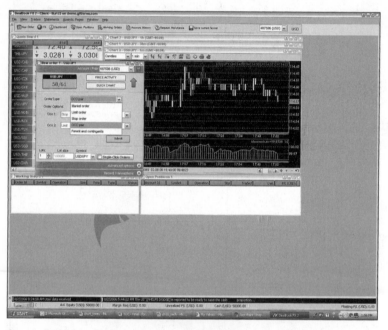

Step 2: Pick the order type you want to place.

Step 3: Set your entry or exit points. You will need to indicate whether you want to buy or sell the currency pair and at what price you want to do that. You can make those changes in the order options section of the new order form.

In the figure that follows, we show you that by clicking on the arrow to the right of Sell you get a drop-down menu that lets you choose whether or not you want to buy or sell the currency. To the left you will see another drop-down menu where you can indicate a limit or stop order. In the middle of that line is where you see the currency price. Next to the currency price is an up and a down arrow. You just click on the arrows to move the price to your desired entry or exit point.

Note that at the top of the following Step 3 figure, the price for the currency pair is shown as 57/60, but below in the currency price box you see 114.57. The quote only shows the last two numbers after the decimal point, indicating the pip spread. Note there is a 3 pip spread in the price quote between 114.57 and 114.60.

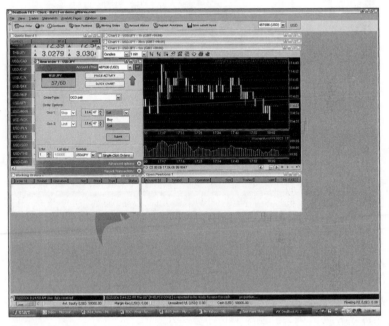

Step 3: Set up your entry or exit points.

Step 4: Indicate number of lots and advanced options. Indicate how many lots you want to buy or sell and the lot size. We've set it to 1 lot of 100,000 in the next figure. We've also opened the advanced options section to set up a time limit for the order. You can see at the bottom of the order screen there are two options for time limit—"Good until Canceled" or "Good until the Close of" and then you are given a list of market close possibilities. We've highlighted Europe/London.

Also note that the price quote for the pair is 74/77. This screenshot was created about 12 hours later and the price for the pair moved from 57/60—a 17 pip difference. We set the final OCO order as a stop order to sell at 114.66 and a limit order to sell at 114.87.

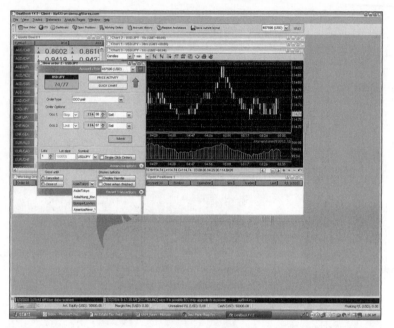

Step 4: You can see that the number of lots to be sold in this image is 1 lot of 100,000. Also, we show you how to select a time limit for the order. In this image, we select Good until Close of the Europe/London market.

Step 5: Confirm your order. Once you're sure you've checked all aspects of your order, hit the submit button. You will get a box asking you to confirm your order. In the Step 5 figure, we show you a confirm order box. You should check the order to be sure that is what you want. If it is, you would hit yes and the order would be placed. If you want to make changes, you would hit no and go back to the order form to make changes.

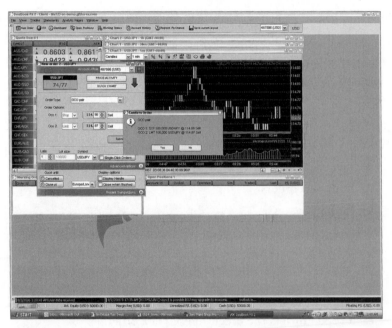

Step 5: This shows a confirmation box. If you click yes, the order will be placed. If you click no, the order will not be placed and you will be able to make changes to the order.

Calculating Profits and Losses

Next, we show you how to calculate your profits or losses. After closing out a position, you take the price you paid to sell the base currency and subtract the price you paid to buy back the base currency, then multiply the difference by the transaction size. That will give you the gain or loss in the currency traded. You would then have to multiply that amount by the conversion rate of that currency to dollars to find out your gain or loss in U.S. dollars.

For example, suppose you bought USD/JPY at 114.66 and sold at 114.57. Also suppose the conversion rate from 1 yen to dollars is .0087. Here is how you would calculate your gain in yen and then convert it to dollars.

- ◆ Step 1: Subtract 114.57–114.66 = .09 pips.

- ◆ Step 2: Multiply .09 × 100,000 = Gain of 9,000 yen

- ◆ Step 3: Multiply 9,000 × .0087 = Gain of $78.30

When you have a profit, you subtract any broker's fees to calculate your profit.

If the numbers were reversed and you had bought yen for 114.57 and sold it for 114.66, then you would have had a loss of 9,000 yen or $78.30.

The Least You Need to Know

- ◆ Be sure you understand the key trading terms before you start placing your orders.

- ◆ You need to use leverage to make money trading currency pairs because currencies are traded in fractions of a cent.

- ◆ Choose a reputable broker that is registered with the CFTC and the NFA.

- ◆ Be certain you know how to place the various order types and how each type impacts the execution of your order.

- ◆ Take the time to learn how to place an order using your broker's software. Practice placing orders using GFT's DealBook® 360.

Chapter

Using Mini Accounts

In This Chapter

- ◆ Taking tiny steps
- ◆ Borrowing too heavily
- ◆ Understanding your risk
- ◆ Recognizing your potential losses

When just getting started with Forex, many people prefer to start slowly by taking tiny steps. You can do that through a mini account.

But be careful. Many mini accounts allow much higher leverage. You can lose your entire deposit in a matter of hours.

In this chapter, we explain how mini accounts work and the dangers of leveraging too much.

Starting Small

A standard lot in Forex is 100,000 units of a specific currency. So if you buy one standard lot of currency with a price of $1.2155, you would control $121,550 of that currency.

$1.2155 × 100,000 = $121,550

Most Forex dealers allow you to buy this lot on a margin account with leverage of 100:1, which translates into a 1 percent margin deposit. So you would need $1,215.50 in your Forex trading account to make this trade.

$121,550 × .01 = $1,215.50

Although this is less than the minimum deposit for standard accounts (minimum deposits typically range from $2,000 to $10,000), if you're new to Forex, that may still be more than you are ready to risk on your first purchase. To make it easier for you as a new trader, and less risky, many brokers and dealers offer what is called a *mini account*.

def•i•ni•tion

A Forex **mini account** allows you to trade a smaller amount of currencies with smaller minimum deposits by using a mini lot. A mini lot is 10,000 units of currency, which is just a tenth of the size of a standard lot of 100,000 units. Mini accounts offer higher leverage, so you can control more currency with a lower deposit.

With a mini account you can buy a mini lot, which is just 10,000 units. So for the same currency exchange example discussed here you would need only a $121.55 security deposit in your account:

$1.2155 × 10,000 = $12,155

$12,155 × .01 = $121.55

You can't make much money trading that small. For example, if the price of the currency moved 100 pips to $1.2255, then it would be worth $12,255. Your profit would be $100. Essentially, with this size lot 1 pip equals $1.

Now, suppose the market moved 100 pips against you to $1.2055, then you would have just $15,055, which would be a loss of $100.

This type of movement in the Forex market can happen over a matter of hours and the amount you deposited can quickly be lost, but at least the loss on a mini account is much less than it would be for a standard lot.

In looking at the same scenario with a standard lot, you would initially control $121,550 with a deposit of $1,215.50. If the market moved in your favor by 100 pips, the lot would be worth:

$$1.2255 \times 100,000 = \$122,550$$

Your profit would be $1,000 less any broker fess.

But, just as quickly, the market could move against by 100 pips to 1.2055, and then your lot would be worth:

$$1.2055 \times 100,000 = \$120,550$$

Your loss would be $1,000 plus any broker fees.

You may not be ready to take that much risk if you're just starting out with Forex trading. You're better off using a mini account initially and making your mistakes by taking less risk. While you won't gain much, use the time trading in a mini account to learn the ropes and test your trading strategies.

By using smaller lot sizes, you'll build up your account slowly. But if you do things right you can build your trading account to a sizeable amount before building the confidence to try your strategies trading standard account sizes.

> **Wealth Builders**
>
> Mini accounts allow you to start small, but don't use that advantage to leverage your purchases too much. While some brokers or dealers allow you to leverage 400:1, don't do it unless you're confident that you know what you are doing. With leverage that high, you can quickly lose more than you spent to initially enter the trade.

Risks of Over-Leveraging

You'll find many brokers out there offer not only mini accounts, but mini accounts with starting deposits of as little as $250 or $300. You may wonder how you could start trading with so little and still be able to avoid putting all your eggs in one basket.

So how can you really learn anything starting with such a small deposit? Brokers or dealers that allow you to start with such a small account also permit you to leverage your money 400:1, which can be very risky. The minimum deposit in this case is calculated by 0.25 percent or by multiplying your lot value by 0.0025.

Using the same numbers again, here's what you would need to have on deposit for a 10,000 unit mini lot when buying a currency worth $1.2155 with 400:1 margin.

$$10,000 \times \$1.2155 \times .0025 = \$30.39$$

Now that looks better if you only deposited $250. You might think you could actually carry out about five or six trades at that level.

But don't get too excited. First think about what happens to your money with that type of leverage if you experience a 100 pip loss. When you leverage 400:1, you still experience the same loss, but you're putting up less money.

You're still in control of the same amount of currency:

$$10,000 \times \$1.2155 = \$12,155$$

If the currency drops 100 pips, it will be worth $1.2055, so you will now be holding currency worth:

$$10,000 \times \$1.2055 = \$12,055$$

So the amount that you spent to buy the currency on margin with just $30.39 has now lost $100 plus. So you've lost more money than you put into the trade.

If you only have $250 on deposit and you experience two losses like this, which can happen very quickly when you are new to trading Forex, your account can be wiped out much more quickly with a 400:1 margin.

Don't Start Too Small!

If you see a margin rate of 400:1, make sure you have a good idea of what you are doing. If you're not ready to put at least $2,500 into starting your Forex trading business, start practicing with a demonstration account and wait until you are ready to make at least that level of commitment.

But don't ever go deeper into your pockets and then use money that you intended for your child's education or your retirement in such a risky venture. You must always be ready to lose all the money in a Forex account, especially when you are first beginning and learning all the tools you'll need—fundamental analysis, technical analysis, and charting.

Take the time to learn and save your risk capital. It will be time well spent to get yourself ready for this opportunity to make a lot of money trading money. But be ready to lose a lot at times, too.

Even the most experienced traders can take a loss when the market moves against their expectations. You can never be immune to periodic losses if you choose to trade Forex.

Some brokers who offer mini accounts will even allow inexperienced traders to open an account using a credit card. This can be extremely risky. Not only can you lose all the money you deposit using a cash advance from your credit card, you would then also be paying high interest rates as you pay back your credit card company, increasing your potential for loss.

Always trade Forex using cash you have deposited. If you use your credit card, you could lose the money you deposited even before you get your credit card bill.

Carefully Check Out Your Loss Potential

When you sign up with a broker, check the small print on your account agreement. Be sure the agreement limits your losses to the amount that you deposit. That means that you should never lose more than you put into your account, except in times of extreme market gapping, when the market is very volatile, such as after a major earthquake.

Before depositing any money, read all the fine print carefully. You must understand your rights and responsibilities, as well as the obligations of your broker.

Capital Cautions

Some brokers promoting mini accounts do so to lure unsuspecting clients into taking more risk than they can truly afford to take. These brokers often don't have the training or the financial ability to even understand how speculative the Forex market truly can be. Don't be one of their victims. Educate yourself fully before beginning to trade.

If you're drawn into the market by high-pressure sales without taking the time to truly learn how to trade Forex successfully, you're doomed to fail and lose all the money you deposit. You could even possibly lose more than you deposit.

Many Forex brokers that offer these low minimum accounts limit their risks but increase yours. Their computer trading software includes built-in liquidation stop losses.

If your trade moves against you, the broker's software is written to automatically limit its risk. When your account falls below a certain level (also known as a margin call, which we discuss in greater depth in Chapter 13), the broker's computer software is programmed to automatically sell your positions to cover your margin call.

When you get a margin call, your holdings can be closed immediately if your account agreement is set up with that type of provision. You could lose your entire account in minutes. Your broker won't lose, though. He's protected himself by putting in these automatic stop losses.

Your losses are locked in because your positions were closed. Your broker is fully protected with the automatic stop losses.

Very high leverage can help you build your small account in a hurry. But it's a double-edged sword. You can also end up burning through your deposit just as quickly if the market moves against you. Concentrate on the size of the risk you are taking on each trade rather than the amount of currency you're going to control.

Test out a number of scenarios based on the way the market may move, just as we did previously. Run the numbers for a 100, 200, or 300 pip gain or loss. Be sure you can handle that level of loss and still be able to trade again. If not, you're probably leveraging too high. Take it slower.

Learn, make your mistakes without taking on too much risk, and give yourself the time to become an experienced, successful Forex trader. You will always find currency to trade. It's much harder to rebuild an account that you've lost completely to trading mistakes.

GFT's Unique Option

Global Forex Trading, the company owned by co-author Gary Tilkin, offers mini accounts with a minimum deposit of $250, and maximum leverage of 400:1.

GFT also offers new Forex traders an option to learn how to trade Forex, with less risk than you'll find in a mini account, called "Base 10 Trading."

Base 10 Trading permits you to trade in multiples of 10. You can buy lots with a minimum of 10,000 instead of the usual 100,000, and you can buy them in multiples of 10. This gives the trader just starting out, as well as the experienced trader, more flexibility to try out different trading strategies, but take a less risky position.

The Least You Need to Know

- You can open a mini Forex account with as little as $250, but make sure you think carefully and manage your leverage wisely.

- You can trade mini Forex lots that are only 10,000 units of a currency rather than a standard lot of 100,000 units.

- If you are going to start small, don't start small with too much leverage that puts you in a position in which you can lose more than you deposit in your account.

Chapter 15

Managed Forex and Trading Systems

In This Chapter

- ◆ Getting help from the professionals
- ◆ Hedging with managed funds
- ◆ Using trading systems or managed accounts

You might be interested in trying Forex trading, but you don't have the time to research and manage a Forex account by yourself. You do have several options—working with a professional manager, opening an account with a hedge fund that specializes in trading Forex, or using a managed trading system.

In this chapter, I review the pros and cons of the managed Forex options.

Professional Forex Managers

Professional Forex managers used to be available only to individuals who had at least $100,000 in their Forex account. Today, some dealers can make arrangements for you to open an account with a professional Forex manager with an initial deposit of as little as $10,000.

Trading Forex requires you to research not only the actual currencies you want to trade, but also all the countries involved in those trades. It can be an enormous task and requires a full-time commitment if you want to do it well.

Picking a well-respected professional Forex manager can help you to develop a well-diversified Forex portfolio using disciplined and proven trading skills. Your manager will have experience seeing profits in both rising and falling markets.

The key of course is to find the right manager. Don't try to do that by researching options completely on your own using the Internet. You'll find hundreds of websites promising professional Forex management, but many are scams. We talk more about the types of scams you may find on the Internet and how to recognize them in Chapter 16.

Seek out advice from trusted friends and associates who have worked with a professional Forex manager and can recommend him highly. Also get recommendations from Forex brokers with whom you are considering opening an account. Research the brokers or dealers before even considering their recommendations through the National Futures Association database (www.nfa.futures.org/basicnet).

Capital Cautions

Don't ever choose a professional Forex manager solely by doing an Internet search, finding an interesting website, and opening a new account online. Be sure to do extensive research on the broker or dealer who has the site as well as the professional Forex manager recommended.

Seek out a professional manager who has years of consistent of Forex trading experience, as well as a solid group of traders working for him. Many top professional Forex managers have developed proprietary technical trading strategies that analyze and predict various trends in the foreign exchange markets.

As you research potential Forex managers, be sure you understand their strategies and whether they might work well for you. For example, a professional manager's experience and research may enable him to spot recurring price patterns that he has learned to take advantage of to make profits.

Most professional Forex managers have complex computer programs that help them manage the funds. These programs automatically monitor holdings for predetermined risk-management factors. These factors will provide a signal for entering and exiting positions at the appropriate time based on the parameters set by the manager.

Research how long the manager usually holds on to his trades. You will find some managers who are day traders closing out all positions at the end of the trading day, some who hold trades one to five days, and some who keep positions open up to 20 days or longer.

Of course, you will have to pay a fee to the manager. A common fee structure is 25 percent of trading profits plus a 2 percent annual management fee. Be prepared to give up a significant portion of your gains, because convenience comes at a cost. Be sure you understand the fees you will pay before opening an account with a professional manager.

Hedge Funds

You can also get into the Forex market by seeking out hedge funds that specialize in trading Forex. Hedge funds are not regulated in the same way as mutual funds, so when choosing a hedge fund, research it carefully. The government regulations for hedge funds are minimal and do little to protect the investor up front. We talk more about cases involving Forex hedge fund scam operators in Chapter 16.

You will most likely need at least $100,000 to buy into a managed hedge fund account. In other words, hedge funds are only for people who can afford to risk a sizeable amount of their cash.

Wealth Builders

You can research hedge funds online through an excellent database called Eurekahedge. Its databases focus on various places around the globe. For example, to find out more information about North American hedge funds, go to www.eurekahedge.com/database/northamerican-hedgefunddirectory.asp.

You will hear stories of people investing hundreds of thousands of dollars, or even millions, in a hedge fund that goes broke and they lose everything. These are highly risky investment vehicles.

Capital Cautions

Don't open an account with a Forex-managed hedge fund with money you can't afford to lose. While the profit potential is high, so is the risk.

Hedge funds, like professional Forex managers, expect significant rewards for their services. Expect fund fees of 25 percent of net profits, which means that you subtract unrealized losses from unrealized gains to find the net profit. They also usually get a 2 percent annual fee for managing the hedge fund portfolio.

The primary benefit of a hedge fund is its diversification, which means the variety of currency pairs and other investments they may hold at any given time. You will find a statement of methodology when you begin researching the hedge fund. That's where you'll discover the fund manager's trading style.

When you get information from the hedge fund, look for details about how many different currency pairs are traded by the fund and in what geographic areas the fund concentrates its research. Be sure the regional areas of interest match your trading goals.

For example, if you want to focus on currency trades in the European market, you don't want to open an account with a hedge fund that focuses on the Asian market with only a small portion of its portfolio in the European markets. In addition, you should find out how long the fund usually holds on to its trades. A fund that closes out its trades daily will likely be more volatile than one that tends to hold winning trades longer.

You should also see a statement about how the manager controls risk and what strategies he uses to minimize risk. While all Forex trading is risky, there are strategies one can take to minimize that risk. You also should look for some discussion about the volatility of the fund. Can you live with those ups and downs? Or will the fund's volatility make you so nervous that you ask to get out at one of the worst times of performance?

Managed Accounts and Trading Systems

Another way to get into the Forex market if you're not ready or able to make the full-time commitment to trade is by using trading systems or managed accounts. Automated trading systems will give you a signal when it's a good time to enter or exit a trade.

Managed Accounts

Managed accounts can be an alternative to hiring a professional manager or buying into a hedge fund. For these types of accounts, you open an account in your name and then take advantage of an automated trading system developed by the account manager.

Managed Forex accounts are not registered as separate investment products with the U.S. Securities and Exchange Commission. As long as Forex is the only asset traded, an account manager doesn't have to officially provide disclosure documents.

Documents you can expect to find with other types of SEC-registered products include information about strategy, audited performance, and fees. Even if the information isn't required, be sure to get it anyway. If you can't get the answers you want, run—don't walk—away.

Some brokers who offer managed accounts require at least a $5,000 deposit. Most others require between $10,000 and $50,000 to open an account.

Many also limit access to the account to once a month on a specified day of the month. You may also be required to give a written notice several days before the last trading day of the month in which you want to withdraw funds in order to be allowed to take out your money.

Capital Cautions

You cannot easily move in and out of many managed accounts. Many limit the frequency with which you can enter or exit the system. Others require advance notice when you want to take out funds. Be sure you understand the rules for withdrawal before you deposit any money in a trading system account.

When you read the fine print on a managed account contract, be certain you understand the fees that you will pay, the minimum deposit you must maintain, and any limitations you might have on withdrawing your money. You don't want to be in a position of not having access to your money when you need it.

Currency Corn
The U.S. Commodity Futures Trading Commission (CFTC) announces at least one case of fraud almost every month involving managed Forex accounts. Investors can lose millions before anyone notices what is happening.
For example, a case involving a Washington State firm named Sterling Forex made headlines in October 2002 for costing Forex investors nearly $1.8 million. The firm was charged with "fraudulent misrepresentation."
Sterling began collecting money from investors for its managed Forex account in 1998 and reported annual profits in excess of 60 percent between the years of 1999 and 2001, when in fact Sterling hadn't even started trading funds until June 2002. By October 2002, when the CFTC closed them down, all investor money was lost. The CFTC said the firm reported falsely on their website that the performance record was audited monthly by a major accounting firm. By the time the CFTC acted, most of the investors' deposits with the firm were lost.

Trading Systems

Trading systems are a way to put your account on automatic pilot and let the system take over. They can be a good option for traders who may be too busy or overwhelmed to actively trade in the Forex market.

Trading systems will offer various trading strategies. Be sure you understand the trading strategies that are automatically programmed into the system you choose. You will find some trading systems that offer aggressive trading strategies, which signal you to take on high risk for a higher profit potential. You'll also find others that are more conservative. While you don't have the potential to make as much with a more conservative system, your losses should also be minimized.

No matter what anyone tells you, no trading system can guarantee profits. Many trading systems signal to you when to buy and sell various Forex pairs. Others automatically handle the trades for you.

You will find promises of incredible trading wins based on hypothetical results. Hypothetical results are not based on a real portfolio trading with real money. They instead are trading simulations using histori- cal price data. The trading system promoter can pick the best results using the best part of historical data for his system. So don't depend on impressive trading results that are based on hypothetical trading data.

Hypothetical trading results are like depending on 20/20 hindsight. Don't we all wish we could do that sometimes? That would give us the chance to correct mistakes by knowing what we know today. Unfortunately, the world doesn't work that way.

You may also see the words that the system is tested using real-time trading. Beware! That doesn't mean that real money was traded. It just means that the system was tested using a live data feed rather than with historical market data.

Fees for trading systems and man- aged accounts vary greatly, but can be as high as 20 percent on trading gains, as well as an annual fee of 1 to 2 percent of your account value. Be certain to read the fine print before signing any contract for a trading system, and make sure you understand the fees you will be charged for the services you will receive.

> **Wealth Builders**
>
> Co-author Gary Tilkin's company, GFT, offers managed trading sys- tems through its website. All systems are developed by professional traders with proven track records of suc- cess. You can read more about what is offered at www.gftforex.com/services/ gftmanagedaccounts.

Managed Forex can be a good alternative if you don't have the time to spend researching the market and learning the trading tools. But you still need to carefully research any of the managers, managed accounts, or trading systems you choose to use. There are many scam artists out there that promise you huge profits with very little risk. Don't believe them. There is no risk-free way to trade Forex.

The Least You Need to Know

♦ You can access professional Forex managers through Forex brokers or dealers that have arrangements with the manager. Call your broker or dealer to find out more about Forex management opportunities.

♦ Hedge funds that specialize in trading Forex give you the opportunity to access professional diversified Forex managers, but be ready to put up at least $100,000 to open an account.

♦ Managed accounts can be a way to take advantage of a professional Forex trader's strategies, but these accounts are not regulated, and you must research the account managers carefully.

♦ Automated trading systems provide a way to use programs developed by professional traders, but be cautious of the promises made by system designers.

Chapter 16

Avoiding Money Fraud

In This Chapter

- ◆ Exposing the lies
- ◆ Researching offers
- ◆ Protecting yourself
- ◆ Seeking advice
- ◆ Resolving disputes

You may hear get-rich-quick promises in late-night television ads or infomercials. You may also see promotions about ways to get rich quick on the Internet by trading in foreign currency.

Don't believe any of them. Forex trading is risky and requires a significant amount of time to learn to do properly.

Avoid getting caught up in Forex fraud schemes. In this chapter, we talk about the common types of fraud claims you might see and what you can do to protect yourself from becoming a victim.

Forex Trading Is Risky. Don't Believe Anyone Who Says It's Not!

Forex scammers use many different types of phrases to lure you in and make you think you can get rich quick. Your parents probably told you if something sounds too good to be true, it probably is. Remember that phrase as you read any offer to trade Forex.

You must be even more aware of scams if you suddenly acquired a large sum of cash from an inheritance, insurance settlement, or retirement funds that could attract fraudulent operators. Once the money is gone, it's very difficult, if not impossible, to recover.

We review some of the key claims you may hear via phone, mail, or e-mail. These claims were gathered by the United States Commodity Futures Trading Commission (CFTC) during their investigations of fraudulent Forex operators.

Claims Predicting Large Profits

Be cautious whenever you hear or read these claims:

+ "Whether the market moves up or down in the currency market, you will make a profit."

+ "Make $1,000 per week, every week."

+ "We are outperforming 90 percent of domestic investments."

+ "The main advantage of the Forex markets is that there is no bear market."

+ "We guarantee you will make at least 30–40 percent rate of return within two months."

You should be careful anytime someone promises you extremely high performance. Usually these claims are false.

Claims Promising No Risk

Anytime someone encourages you to trade Forex with a claim that there is little or no financial risk, it's false. Here are some common claims the CFTC has seen in fraudulent scams:

- ◆ "With a $10,000 deposit, the maximum you can lose is $200 to $250 per day."

- ◆ "We promise to recover any losses you have."

- ◆ "Your investment is secure."

Any attempt made by a company to downplay the risks you will take trading Forex is likely a scam. Don't trust anyone who tells you that the written risk disclosure statement you see in the mailing you received or on their website you are reading is just a required formality of a government agency.

You must accept that the currency markets are volatile and risks can be substantial, especially for inexperienced customers. Scammers look for unsuspecting folks who will deposit their money and quickly lose it. The scammers protect themselves from losses by putting automatic stops in as your money disappears. In Chapter 13, we talk more about how Forex trading is done on margin and the risks involved.

Avoid Firms That Promise Trading on the "Interbank Market"

Any firms that claim you can trade in the "interbank market" (that's where the big boys play) or that they will do it for you (other than a reputable managed account) are likely setting you up for a fall. Unregulated, fraudulent currency trading firms often tell their potential customers that their funds are traded in the "interbank market" to get you the best prices.

The only types of firms that do trade money on the interbank market are banks, investment banks, and large corporations. You won't be able to trade, and anyone who claims you can is not telling you the truth—unless, of course, you are planning to trade using the services of a major bank or investment bank, and with a very significant amount of capital. As long as you are working directly with a well-known bank, you are likely trading with an institution that is regulated by the government and not a scam artist.

Be Cautious About Trading Online

While you will find reputable firms that do offer online trading services, be sure you know a lot more about the firm you will be using for online trading other than what is on their website. Once you send funds electronically, it will likely be impossible to get them back if you later find out that the company is a fraudulent operator.

> **Capital Cautions**
>
> An enticing Internet site can look very professional. But remember it can cost an Internet advertiser just pennies per day to reach a potential audience of millions of people. Fraudulent currency trading firms have learned that the Internet is an inexpensive and effective way to reach a large pool of potential customers.

Many of the fraudulent Forex Internet scammers are not even located in the United States. You may not even find an address or other information identifying their nationality or location. If you do transfer funds to a foreign firm, you have even less of a chance to recover your money. Be sure you know exactly where your funds will be held when you open an account.

Scams Targeting Ethnic Minorities

Some Forex scammers find that a great way to get new customers is to target people in ethnic communities. The CFTC found that people in Russian, Chinese, and Indian immigrant communities are targeted through advertisements in their ethnic newspapers and through television "infomercials" on stations that serve those communities.

> **Capital Cautions**
>
> Sophisticated fraud operators may give you a beautifully designed glossy brochure with impressive-looking charts. Don't depend on it. The information may be false. Always research a firm's claims no matter how good the information looks.

One common scam used in these communities is to advertise as though the company is offering you a "job opportunity" for an "account executive" to trade foreign currencies. When you get to the job, you find out that you must use your own money for trading. You likely will also be encouraged to recruit family and friends. You could be lured into a trap not only to lose your own money, but to encourage your family members and friends to lose theirs.

Don't Open an Account If You Can't Check a Firm's Background

Any firm that won't give you enough information to check their background is probably a fraudulent operator. Don't just accept the information you're given; be sure to carefully check it all out with the regulatory agencies at the federal and state level. We talk more about how to do that in the following section on regulatory agencies. We also provide full details about the regulatory agencies in Appendix C.

When you do get information about a firm's background, don't depend on verbal statements you get from its employees. Be sure you get all the information in written form.

If you are not able to verify the information you are given, it's a sure sign you're dealing with a questionable firm. Don't do business with any firm that you can't prove is legitimate.

Don't Make Quick Decisions

A favorite tactic of many Forex scammers is to tell you by phone or e-mail that you must respond within a number of minutes or hours in order to get the deal promised. Don't fall for that tactic.

You should always take the time to research the firm that approached you. You should be sure that the firm is legitimate and one that you would be comfortable using as your broker.

Also, you should always research any tip or idea independently yourself. If you don't understand the tip or why it's worth acting upon, don't take the action.

Get Everything in Writing

You may hate to read the fine print, but be sure you get everything that is promised to you in writing. Read all documentation carefully and be sure that you understand what is being said.

Before opening an account, you should get a contract that spells out all the trading rules, referred to as the customer or account agreement. You should also get a risk disclosure statement that clearly spells out the risks of trading Forex.

In the customer or account agreement, you should find details about the laws and regulations under which the firm operates, the deposit requirements, details about trading on margin, and what happens if your account falls short. You should get information on how trades will be liquidated.

You should also get a full listing of services provided and any fees and charges for those services. Be sure that you understand all fees and the basis for each of these charges.

If you do plan to trade online, there will likely be a separate agreement for electronic order entry and access that spells out how to access your account online and how it will be managed.

Your entire relationship with your Forex broker will be governed by this customer or account agreement. Be sure you understand your rights and responsibilities, as well as the firm's rights and responsibilities, before signing anything.

If you don't understand something, ask about it and be sure that you do understand all provisions before signing the document. If the answer seems to differ from what you are seeing, be sure you get all promises in writing.

Avoid Any Money Manager That Won't Give You a Performance Track Record

If you choose to go with a money manager to handle your Forex account, you should always seek as much information as you can about their past performance. But be aware that the information you receive may not always be reliable, and can be very difficult to verify. Fraudulent money managers have been found to indicate that their performance track record is audited by an independent accounting firm, even though that information in itself is fraudulent.

Money managers are not required to provide this information, but be leery of any that refuse to give you information about its performance track record. And, of course, always look for a money manager with a long history of a reliable positive performance record.

 Wealth Builders

Remember that anything a salesperson promises may not actually be honored if you don't get it in writing. If a salesperson hedges on putting something in writing, the claim likely is not true.

Check with Regulatory Agencies

Before you even open an account, here are the key steps you should take to research the company to make sure it's legitimate.

CFTC

Your first stop should be the CFTC's consumer protection web page. You can access that by going to www.cftc.gov and clicking on the link to consumer protection. There you will find the most current advisories on Forex fraud operations that the CFTC is investigating. You'll also get links to consumer advisories, as well as be able to report information about any questionable offers that you receive.

National Futures Association (NFA)

Your next stop should be the website of the National Futures Association. There you can use the NFA's Background Affiliation Status Information Center—BASIC—(www.nfa.futures.org/basicnet) to find out whether the company is registered with the CFTC and is a member of the NFA.

You are much safer working with a firm that is registered with the CFTC and is a member of the NFA. These firms must follow government regulations, and you have access to account discrepancy resources if problems arise (we talk more about dispute resolution soon).

Capital Cautions

Firms not registered with the CFTC could be questionable. Registration is not required to open a Forex trading firm.

You should also check whether or not there has been disciplinary action against the firm. You can find out a firm's or an individual's status and disciplinary record using the BASIC database at NFA's website.

Contact State Authorities

If you've had no success finding the information you need, you can contact your state authorities. You should also research the firm's background information further to be sure there aren't any problems noticed by your state's agencies. Here are a few contacts you should make:

♦ Your state's Securities Commissioner, which you can find online using the database at the North American Securities Administrators Association (www.nasaa.org/QuickLinks/ContactYourRegulator.cfm).

♦ Your state attorney general's consumer protection bureau, which you can find online using the database at the website of the National Association of Attorneys General www.naag.org/. In the middle of the page you'll see a drop-down menu you can use to locate the attorney general for your state. You'll then be able to get to his or her information page where you'll find a link to the attorney general's consumer protection website.

♦ The Better Business Bureau. As with any company you plan to do business with, it's a good idea to check with the Better Business Bureau to find out if any claims have been filed against the firm. On the national Better Business Bureau website (www.bbb.org) you will find links to access the national database of businesses, as well as information to contact your local Better Business Bureau or to access its website.

If the firm you are researching is located in another state, you should also contact the securities commissioner, attorney general, and Better Business Bureau for the state in which the business is located. There may be complaints filed in the firm's home state that are not known by your state officials.

Seek Professional Advice from an Independent Third Party

It's always a good idea to seek advice from an independent third party that won't benefit financially from your decision to do business with a firm, especially when you are thinking of risking a lot of money. If you do want to get involved in Forex trading, talk with your local banker or accountant. He may be able to recommend a number of good firms to work with or possibly even a contact within your own bank.

You don't have to work with your bank, but it can't hurt to sit down and talk with someone as you gather information about your Forex trading options.

Resolving Problems with Your Forex Account

You may from time to time find that you are having a problem resolving an issue with your Forex broker or dealer. Your first step should be to try to resolve the issue directly with the firm, but if you are not successful you may be able to seek the help of the CFTC and NFA in resolving your dispute.

NFA Dispute Resolution Program

The NFA offers a dispute resolution program to help customers and members of the NFA to resolve disputes. As long as the firm you are dealing with is a member of the NFA, you can seek their assistance. That's one of the key reasons to do your research up front and only work with Forex trading companies that are members of the NFA.

Wealth Builders

You can get information about NFA's Dispute Resolution program by calling 800-621-3570. You can also read more about the program at www. nfa.futures.org. You will find a link to the Dispute Resolution program at the top of the page.

The NFA offers both arbitration and mediation. Arbitration involves a process where the NFA member and the client present their arguments and any supporting evidence to an impartial third party or panel. The impartial third party or panel decides how the matter should be resolved.

Mediation involves a process where the two parties in dispute work with an independent third party called a mediator to resolve the dispute in a way that is mutually agreeable. The mediator does not decide who is right or wrong, but tries to get both parties to come to an agreement.

CFTC Reparations Program

The CFTC offers a reparations program for resolving disputes, which you can find online at www.cftc.gov/cftc/cftccomplaints.htm. This program serves people who have suffered a loss as a result of a commodity law violation. Currency is one of the many commodities the CFTC regulates. In order for the CFTC to get involved, the alleged violation must have been committed by a futures professional, which includes Forex brokers and dealers, provided they have registered with the CFTC. There are three types of reparations proceedings:

♦ Voluntary proceedings, which cost $50 to file, are the quickest. These do not involve hearings or appeals. Complaints are dealt with solely on the basis of written submissions and any supporting evidence provided by the parties involved. If you choose to use this method, you do waive your right to appeal. All parties must consent to the rules of a voluntary proceeding before a case can go forward using this method. The decision of a voluntary proceeding cannot be appealed. There will be no factual findings or a discussion of how the decision was reached when a person choosing to file using voluntary proceedings and the parties involved accept this type of proceeding. There is no dollar limit in a voluntary proceeding.

- Summary proceedings, which cost $125 to file, are used to resolve claims for $30,000 or less. These proceedings are conducted orally by conference call if a judge decides a hearing is needed. The results of a summary judgment can be appealed. The initial decision will include factual findings and a discussion of the basis for the decision. The party that loses in the summary proceedings has the right to appeal the decision first to the full CFTC commission and then to the Federal Court of Appeals.

- Formal proceedings, which cost $250 to file, are used to resolve claims over $30,000 and involve an in-person hearing. The initial decision can be appealed and will include factual findings and a discussion of the basis for the legal conclusions. The party that loses in the formal proceedings has the right to appeal the decision first to the full CFTC commission and then to the Federal Court of Appeals.

In any of these types of proceedings, the customers can seek actual damages, which include all out-of-pocket trading losses. If the customer wins, he can recover his losses as well as the filing fee. Customers may represent themselves or be represented by a lawyer.

You must file your reparations complaint within two years of the date that your cause of action occurs. This means two years from the date you know or should have known that there was wrongdoing. If you think you have been harmed by a violation of commodity laws, you should file with the CFTC as soon as possible to protect your rights.

You may be wondering what you need to file a complaint. Here are the key points on the CFTC's checklist:

- Was the broker, dealer, or firm registered with the CFTC at the time of the alleged violations? If you did your research before opening the account, you should have a record of this.

- Does the issue in question fall under the jurisdiction of the reparations program? Did you suffer a loss as a result of commodity law violation?

- List the names, addresses, and telephone numbers of each individual firm alleged in the complaint.

- ◆ Provide a complete description of your case including a chronological account of the acts involved, the names of the persons who committed each act, the date and place of each act, and the way in which these acts harmed you.

- ◆ Provide an explanation for the amount of damages you are seeking and how you calculated those damages.

- ◆ Attach all supporting documents, such as account statements and account opening documents.

- ◆ Include a statement about other legal actions you may already have taken, including any arbitration proceeding or civil court litigation you may have filed.

- ◆ Include a statement indicating if any of the parties named are in pending receivership or bankruptcy proceedings.

You will also need to state under which type of proceeding you are filing—voluntary, summary, or formal—and pay the required filing fee.

If you do have a problem with an account, provided you've done your research up front you should be protected. Be sure to find out whether the broker or dealer you plan to use is registered with the CFTC and a member of the NFA. This research will be very valuable later and put you will in a strong position to protect yourself. If you failed to do this research, you may be out of luck trying to get your money back from a fraudulent operator.

Don't Trade More Than You Can Afford to Lose

Rule number one for Forex trading is to never risk more than you can afford to lose. We know that we've said this numerous times in the book, but it is the most important thing for you to remember as you enter the exciting world of Forex trading.

The Least You Need to Know

- Familiarize yourself with the typical fraudulent claims and avoid getting lured in by them.

- Read everything carefully before you sign it and make sure that all promises you receive verbally are made in writing.

- Carefully research any firm you plan to work with through both federal and state agencies.

- You can get help if you are harmed by a Forex broker or dealer that is registered with the CFTC and a member of the NFA, so be sure you are dealing with someone who is registered.

Appendix A

Glossary

American terms The phrase is used in the United States, and refers to a direct quotation for U.S. dollars per one unit of the foreign currency.

arbitration This involves a process during which an impartial third party hears the arguments between two parties and reviews any supporting evidence. He then decides how the matter should be resoled.

ask This is the price at which the Forex market maker will be willing to sell a currency pair, and at which a customer can buy the pair.

balance of payments This measures the flow of money into and out of a particular country to other countries. Pieces of this calculation include a country's exports and imports of goods and services, as well as the transfer of financial capital. The balance of payments is basically the summary of all economic transactions between a country and all other countries during a particular period, usually a quarter (three months) or a year.

Bank for International Settlements (BIS) An international organization based in Basel, Switzerland, that serves as a bank for the world's central banks. It fosters international monetary and financial cooperation by promoting discussion and policy analysis among central banks and the international financial community. It also conducts economic and monetary research.

Bank of Japan Financial Network System (BOJ-NET)   The BOJ-NET processes transactions involving the Japanese yen and the Bank of Japan and other Japanese financial institutions through its online network. The Bank of Japan started developing BOJ-NET in 1982 and began its foreign exchange yen settlement service in 1989.

bar chart   This shows the highs and lows for the currency during the time period selected. Each bar on the chart represents one time period.

base currency   This is the underlying or fixed currency. For example, in European terms, the U.S. dollar is the base currency because it is the currency in the transaction that is fixed to one unit. When you hear a quote, the base currency is stated first.

bear market   This type of market is one in which the overall market is trending down.

bid   This is the price at which the Forex market maker would be willing to buy a currency.

Bretton Woods Accord   This accord established a system of international monetary management with rules for commercial and financial relations among the world's major industrial nations after World War II in July 1944. The accord died in 1971 when then-President Richard Nixon single-handedly closed the gold market and made the dollar no longer convertible to gold directly.

bull market   This type of market is one in which the overall market is trending up.

candlestick charts   These charts originated in Japan over 300 years ago. In these charts, a little box forms representing the time periods instead of just bar lines. The top of the box is the opening price for the period the bottom of the box is the closing price. On most candlesticks, you'll also see a line above and below the box. The line above the box shows you the high during the period and the line below the box shows you the low.

carry trade   This is a foreign exchange strategy where a trader sells a certain currency with a relatively low interest rate and uses the funds to purchase a different currency yielding a higher interest rate. The trader attempts to benefit from the difference in the two rates.

CHAPS   CHAPS is an electronic system for settling same-day transactions involving the British pound sterling with the United Kingdom Clearing Banks. Payments are individually and continuously processed through CHAPS throughout the day, in real time.

CHIPS   This is a private bank-owned settlement system for clearing large value payments of the U.S. dollar. CHIPS processes over 285,000 payments a day with a gross value of $1.4 trillion. It serves the largest banks from around the world, representing 19 countries worldwide. CHIPS has been processing payments for U.S. corporate and financial institutions for over 35 years. Today it processes over 95 percent of the U.S. dollar cross-border payments.

CLS   CLS Group was founded in 1997 to create the first global settlement system with the goal of eliminating settlement risk in the foreign exchange market. The CLS service, offered by CLS Bank International, is supported by over 70 of the world's largest banking and financial institutions. CLS is a unique real-time process enabling simultaneous FX settlement across the globe, eliminating the settlement risk caused by delays arising from time-zone differences.

Commodity Futures Trading Commission (CFTC)   A U.S. government entity that protects market users and the public from fraud, manipulation, and abusive practices related to the sale of commodity and financial futures and options. The Commission's mission also includes fostering open, competitive, and financially sound futures and options markets.

counterparty   Every foreign currency exchange involves a pair of currencies traded between two parties. In order to trade a currency pair, you need to have a counterparty, such as a dealer or broker, who is willing to trade with you. For example, if someone wants to trade U.S dollars for euros, one party will need to be holding the euros and one party will need to be holding the dollars in order to trade.

DAX 100   The DAX 100 is an index of the 100 most heavily traded stocks in the German stock market.

derivatives   These are a type of financial instrument that's value is dependent upon another instrument, such as a commodity, bond, stock, or currency. Futures and options are two types of financial derivatives.

Dow Jones Industrial Index (DOW) The DOW is the most widely used indicator of the overall condition of the stock market, but it only tracks 30 actively traded blue chip stocks. The stocks tracked are picked by the editors of *The Wall Street Journal.* The DOW index was founded in 1896 by Charles Dow.

economic indicators These include any variable that gives you an idea of where the market may be headed, such as new employment statistics or trading balances.

electronic funds transfer (EFT) This is a system where money is transferred from one bank account directly to another without any paper money changing hands. If you use direct deposit for your paycheck, that is a form of an EFT. Most Forex trading is done using an EFT.

EURO 1 EURO 1 is a large-value payment system for euro payments managed by the EBA Clearing Company, which was set up by the Euro Banking Association (EBA). The EBA is a cooperative undertaking between EU-based commercial banks and EU branches of non-EU credit institutions. Currently more than 70 participating banks from the 15 member states of the European Union (EU) and five non-EU countries participate in the system. EURO 1 handles credit transfers and direct debits. Payments are processed throughout the day. Balances are settled at the end of the day via a settlement account at the European Central Bank.

European terms This phrase refers to a direct quotation for someone in Europe from their currency per one unit of U.S. dollar.

Federal Open Market Committee (FOMC) This committee of the U.S. Federal Reserve is a group of 19 people plus about 40 staffers. The 7 members of the Federal Reserve Board and 12 presidents of the Federal Reserve Banks make up the committee. When the committee takes a vote only 12 of the people can vote, the 7 Federal Reserve Board members, the president of the New York Fed and 4 of the other 11 Federal Reserve Bank presidents. Voting rights rotate among the bank presidents.

Fedwire The Fedwire Funds Service provides a real-time gross settlement system (RTGS) to the more than 9,500 participants in the Federal Reserve System that maintain a reserve or clearing account with a Federal Reserve Bank. You must have an account with a Federal Reserve bank to use Fedwire. Participants use Fedwire to handle large-value, time-critical payments, such as payments for the settlement of interbank purchases and sales of federal funds; the purchase, sale, and financing of securities transactions; the disbursement or repayment of loans; and the settlement of real estate transactions. Payment instructions can be given online or by telephone.

fixed exchange rate   This is a type of exchange rate regime where a currency's value is matched to the value of an individual country's currency or a basket of other countries' currencies.

floating exchange rate   This is an exchange rate regime where the value of a currency fluctuates according to the foreign exchange market, rather than being pegged to a specific commodity (such as gold) or a specific currency (such as the U.S. dollar).

Forex   A shortened version of foreign exchange. Commonly used to refer to the foreign exchange trading market.

forward transactions   With this transaction, you trade one currency for another on a pre-agreed date at some time in the future, but it must be three or more days after the deal date. The forward transaction is a straightforward single purchase or sale of one currency for another.

FTSE 100   This stock index tracks the top 100 stocks on the London Stock Exchange and is similar to the S&P 500. The index is co-owned by the *Financial Times* daily newspaper of London and the London Stock Exchange.

fundamental analysis   Using this type of analysis, one collects data about what is happening in the economy and tries to understand how these economic conditions impact the current value of a particular currency, as well as predict what might happen to the currency's future value. Many things can impact the state of the economy, including monetary policy set by government agencies, capital and trade flows, production, and employment (or unemployment). Understanding these key economic indicators and how they impact the value of money is critical for currency traders.

GDP or **Gross Domestic Product**   This is the market value of all final goods and services produced within a country during a specified period of time.

International Bank for Reconstruction and Development   This
bank initially served as a vehicle for the reconstruction of Europe and
Japan during World War II. Today it fosters economic growth in developing countries in Africa, Asia, and Latin America, as well as the post-
Socialist states of Eastern Europe and the former Soviet Union.

International Monetary Fund   The IMF oversees the global financial system. It monitors exchange rates and balance of payments for
foreign exchange transactions, and provides technical and financial
assistance when requested by individual member counties.

laws of supply and demand   The law of supply states that as price
rises, the quantity supplied rises; as price falls, the quantity supplied
falls. The law of demand states as price falls, the quantity demanded
rises; as price rises, the quantity of demand falls. When supply and
demand are in balance, that means at a certain price and quantity, the
amount the buyer wants to buy is equal to what the seller wants to sell.

limit order   This type of order allows you to specify a price at which
you want to buy or sell the currency. If you are looking to buy a currency, you would place a limit order specifying that you will buy the
currency at a specific price or lower. If you are looking to sell a currency, you would place a limit order specifying that you will sell the
currency at a specific price or higher.

line chart   This chart is created by plotting one price point of a currency over a specified period of time. The line is made by connecting
the dots of each of these plotted points.

managed float regime   This is a currency regime in which the exchange rates fluctuate from day to day, but a central bank attempts to
influence the country's exchange rates by buying and selling currencies.
This is also known as a "dirty float."

margin   This is the amount of money deposited by a customer that is
required to be deposited to the broker or dealer. Margin is a percentage
of the Forex position value.

margin call   This is a broker or dealer's demand on a customer to
deposit additional funds into his or her account. Margin calls are made
to bring a customer's account up to a minimum level.

market maker   In the foreign exchange world, a market maker is a
bank or Forex dealer that provides publicly quoted prices for specific

currency pairs. Market makers add liquidity, and provide a two-sided market. International banks serve as market makers for more than 70 percent of the foreign exchange market. Retail, or individual, customers typically go through licensed Forex dealing firms that act as market makers, because these firms can access the prices and liquidity of the international banks, while providing individuals with market access.

market order This is the simplest and most basic order you can place. It is an order to buy or sell a financial instrument immediately at the best possible price.

market sentiment This reflects the general mood surrounding the currency market. Understanding this general mood will help you develop a plan based on the expected behavior of the market, which can be critical to developing a good trading plan.

mediation This involves a process where two parties try to come to a mutually acceptable agreement with the help of a third party.

mini account This type of Forex account allows you to buy a smaller amount of currency using a mini lot. A mini lot is 10,000 units of currency, which is just a tenth the size of a standard lot of 100,000 units. Mini accounts typically have smaller minimum deposit requirements, and offer higher leverage.

Nasdaq Composite The Nasdaq Composite Index tracks primarily technology stocks, so it is not a good indicator of the broader stock market, but is a good indicator of what is happening in growth stocks. The index dates back to 1971, when the Nasdaq stock exchange was first created.

National Futures Association (NFA) This is the industry-wide, self-regulatory organization for the U.S. futures industry that develops rules, programs, and services to safeguard market integrity, protect investors and help its members meet regulatory responsibilities.

Nikkei index The Nikkei index is the most respected index of Japanese stocks. The index is calculated using Japan's top 225 blue-chip companies on the Tokyo Stock Exchange. Many think of the Nikkei as the equivalent of the Dow index in the United States. It was even named the Nikkei Dow Jones Stock Average from 1975 to 1985. The index was starting by Japan's leading business newspaper, *The Nikkei*, in 1950.

payment When carrying out a foreign exchange transaction, the payment involves giving instructions regarding the value of the transaction.

pip This is the smallest amount that a currency pair can move in price. This is similar to a "tick" on the stock market.

PNS PNS is a hybrid settlement system. Participants can set bilateral limits. Transactions are settled in real time if there is sufficient liquidity in the participant's account and if bilateral limits are met. Otherwise, transactions are queued.

position This is the amount of currency you own or owe in your trading account.

POPS POPS is a real-time system operated by the participating banks on a decentralized basis in Finland. It is the Finnish TARGET component BoF-RTGS. At the end of the day a settlement is made, thereby zeroing any remaining bilateral obligations.

real-time gross settlement system (RTGS) This is the continuous settlement of payments on an individual order basis. RTGS is a system for large-value interbank funds transfers. Settlement risk is minimized because interbank settlements occur throughout the day rather than just at the end of the day.

resistance When using technical analysis, resistance is a price point above the current market price at which sellers decide to sell. It is always the upper trading range boundary. When a currency pair hits the resistance point, buyers are losing interest in buying because the price is too high and sellers must lower their price in order to find buyers.

settlement When carrying out a foreign exchange transaction, the settlement involves the actual clearing of the funds based on the payment instructions.

Smithsonian Agreement This international agreement was made in 1971 when the Group of Ten devalued the dollar to $38 per ounce of gold with trading allowed up to 2.25 percent above or below that value. Dollars could not be used to convert directly to gold.

spot Forex market This is a market in which the currency is bought and sold for cash and delivered immediately.

spot rate   This is the current market price, also known as the benchmark price.

spot transaction   This is the simplest type of transaction in the world of foreign exchange. It is simply the exchange of one currency for another.

stop order   This type of order will automatically be executed when your price is hit. When the price is hit, the order becomes a market order and will be executed immediately.

stop-limit order   This type of order uses the benefits of both a stop order and a limit order. If you place a stop order, but are worried that the market may move too quickly for the order to be executed in time, then you can include a limit order as part of the stop order. When you use a stop-limit order, the stop becomes a limit order rather than a market order and won't be executed unless your broker or dealer can get the price you specified or better.

support   In technical analysis, support is a price point below the current market price where buying occurs. It is always the lower trading range boundary. When the price drops to the support level, then buyers start to buy to stop the price from dropping any lower.

swap   An FX swap allows you to exchange one currency for another and then re-exchange back to the currency you first held.

TARGET   TARGET is the RTGS system for the euro and was created by interconnecting two key settlements systems—the national euro real-time gross settlements system and the European Central Bank payment mechanism. It is used for the settlement of Central Bank operations, large-value euro interbank transfers as well as other euro payments. It provides real-time processing and settlement in central bank money. TARGET stands for **T**rans-European **A**utomated **R**eal-time **G**ross settlement **E**xpress **T**ransfer system.

technical analysis   This looks at the historical price movements and patterns of currencies. Technical analysts believe that by tracking a currency's historical price movements, you can spot trends and predict future price movements.

terms currency   This currency is the foreign currency that is being quoted as a pair to the base currency.

UK gilt   A government bond similar to U.S. treasury bonds.

World Bank   This bank provides financial and technical assistance to developing countries around the world. The bank is owned by 184 member countries and works to reduce global poverty and improve the living standards of people in developing countries. The bank provides low-interest loans, as well as interest-free credit and grants to developing countries for education, health, infrastructure, communications, and other purposes.

Websites

Key Regulatory Agencies

The two primary Forex regulators are as follows:

Commodity Futures Trading Commission (www.cftc.gov) is a U.S. government entity that protects market users and the public from fraud, manipulation, and abusive practices related to the sale of commodity and financial futures and options. The Commission's mission also includes fostering open, competitive, and financially sound futures and options markets.

National Futures Association (www.nfa.futures.org) is a self-regulatory body for the futures industry that was given its authority by the Commodity Futures Trading Commission (CFTC). All Forex dealers and market makers must be registered with the NFA. You can find out if your broker is affiliated with the NFA by using the National Futures Association's Background Affiliation Status Information Center at www.nfa.futures.org/basicnet.

In addition to these two primary Forex regulators, you can get help at the state or local level:

National Association of Attorneys General (www.naag.org) provides links to your state attorney general's consumer protection bureau. In the middle of the page you'll see a drop down menu you can use to locate the attorney general for your state. You'll then be able to get to his or her information page where you will find a link to the attorney general's consumer protection website.

North American Securities Administrators Association (www.nasaa.org/QuickLinks/ContactYourRegulator.cfm) provides links to your state's securities commissioner.

Better Business Bureau (www.bbb.org) can help you research any business you plan to work with. On the national Better Business Bureau website you will find links to access the national database of businesses, as well as information to contact your local Better Business Bureau or to access its website.

Key News Sources About Currency

Here are the major currency-related news media outlets:

Bloomberg (www.bloomberg.com) is the leading global provider of financial news. It does have a radio and a television station, which is great if your local cable provider includes it in your package, but if not, you can always access its information online.

Business Week (www.businessweek.com) is an excellent weekly business news magazine.

CNN Money (money.cnn.com) is a good source to find information about investment waves to locate your next best trading opportunity.

Financial Times (www.ft.com) provides an excellent overview of the financial news from a European perspective (based in London). When trading foreign currency, it's critical to understand the news from a global perspective. You can find excellent coverage of currency trends in the *Financial Times* (http://news.ft.com/markets/currencies) currency section.

The Wall Street Journal (www.wsj.com) is the most respected daily business newspaper. You do need to buy a subscription to read the articles online, but you can get one for as low as $99. The expense is well worth it, no matter what type of trading you plan to do.

In addition to the major news media, several key Forex websites can help keep you informed about money trends:

FX Street (www.fxstreet.com) focuses entirely on Forex news. There you will find breaking news about various currencies as well as upcoming economic events and economic indicators. FX Street provides forecasts on key currencies from numerous analysts at www.fxstreet.com/nou/grups_continguts/senseframesboa2.asp. You can find forecasts and commentary about the U.S. dollar, the euro, the British pound, the Japanese yen, the Australian dollar, the Canadian dollar, the Swiss franc, and the Chinese renminbi.

FX World Trade (www.fxworldtrade.com) focuses on commentary and data for five key currencies and how the currencies are trading with the U.S. dollar, including the Japanese yen, the Canadian dollar, the euro, the Swiss franc, and the British pound. It also provides forecasts regarding key economic news that could impact the value of the currencies.

Global Forex Trading (www.gftforex.com/resources) provides resources on its website to help you trade. The website includes commentary and forecasts from some of the leading experts in the Forex market, and an economic calendar. This site also provides real-time prices for currency exchange rates.

U.S. State Department (www.state.gov/r/pa/ei/bgn/) provides a good summary about the political conditions and the economy of countries in the "Background Notes" section.

Exchanges for Options on Foreign Currencies

Chicago Mercantile Exchange (www.cme.com)

New York Board of Trade (www.nybot.com)

Philadelphia Stock Exchange (www.phlx.com)

U.S.-Based Forex Settlement Systems

CHIPS (www.chips.org) is a private bank-owned settlement system for clearing large value payments of the U.S. dollar. It serves the largest banks from around the world, representing 19 countries worldwide. Today it processes over 95 percent of the U.S. dollar cross-border payments.

Fedwire (frbservices.org) provides a real-time gross settlement system (RTGS) to the more than 9,500 participants in the Federal Reserve System that maintain a reserve or clearing account with a Federal Reserve Bank.

European Forex Settlement Systems

CHAPS (www.bankofengland.co.uk/markets/paymentsystems) is an electronic system for settling same-day transactions involving the British pound sterling with the United Kingdom Clearing Banks.

EURO 1 (www.abe.org) is a large-value payment system for euro payments managed by the EBA Clearing Company, which was set up by the Euro Banking Association (EBA).

PNS (www.banque-france.fr) is a hybrid settlement system. End-of-day balances are credited to the participants' settlement accounts at the Banque de France.

POPS (www.bof.fi) is a real-time system operated by the participating banks on a decentralized basis in Finland. It is the Finnish TARGET component BoF-RTGS. At the end of the day a settlement is made, thereby zeroing any remaining bilateral obligations.

TARGET (www.ecb.int/paym/target) is the RTGS system for the euro and was created by interconnecting two key settlement systems—the national euro real-time gross settlement system and the European Central Bank payment mechanism.

Other Forex Settlement Systems

BOJ-NET (www.boj.or.jp), the Bank of Japan Financial Network System, processes transactions involving the Japanese yen and the Bank of Japan and other Japanese financial institutions through its online network.

CLS Group (www.cls-services.com/cls_bank) was founded in 1997 to create the first global settlement system with the goal of eliminating settlement risk in the foreign exchange market.

Central Banks

The following is a list of central banks around the world:

- ◆ Reserve Bank of Australia (www.rba.gov.au)
- ◆ Bank of Canada (www.bankofcanada.ca/en/monetary/target.html)
- ◆ Czech National Bank (www.cnb.cz/en/index.html)
- ◆ Bank of England (www.bankofengland.co.uk)
- ◆ European Central Bank (www.ecb.int/home/html/index.en.html)
- ◆ Hong Kong Monetary Authority (www.info.gov.hk/hkma/eng/ currency/link_ex/index.htm)
- ◆ Bank of Japan (www.boj.or.jp/en/)
- ◆ Reserve Bank of New Zealand (www.rbnz.govt.nz)
- ◆ South African Reserve Bank (www.resbank.co.za/navigate.htm)
- ◆ Swiss National Bank (www.snb.ch/e/index3.html)
- ◆ Central Bank of the Republic of Turkey (www.tcmb.gov.tr/yeni/ eng/index.html)
- ◆ U.S. Federal Reserve (www.federalreserve.gov)

Other key web sources of the U.S. Federal Reserve include:

- ◆ Federal Reserve activities related to foreign exchange are handled at the New York Federal Reserve (www.newyorkfed.org/ education/fx/foreign.html).
- ◆ The Fed's Beige Book (www.federalreserve.gov/FOMC/ BeigeBook/2006/) summarizes economic conditions in the United States.

♦ The Fed's Fred (Federal Reserve Economic Data) (research. stlouisfed.org/fred2) database is an excellent resource with all current economic indicators.

Money Forums

Elite Trader (www.elitetrader.com) provides an online community for discussion about not only Forex, but also stock, options, and futures trading.

MoneyTec Traders (www.moneytec.com) is a discussion forum that serves as a resource to help Forex traders become better traders. You can meet fellow traders from around the world and learn more about Forex trading, as well as discuss trading ideas, techniques, and strategies.

Trading Platforms

In addition to co-author Gary Tilkin's DealBook® 360, which you can download from the CD included with this book or at www.gftforex. com/software/dealbookfx/download.asp, here are some other reputable trading platforms you can try out:

♦ **Capital Market Services** (www.cmsfx.com). You can open an account with US$200. Languages available are Arabic, Chinese, English, French, Italian, German, Japanese, Korean, Russian, and Spanish.

♦ **Forex Capital Markets** (www.fxcm.com). You can open an account with US$2,000. Languages available include Afrikaans, Arabic, Chinese, Dutch/Flemish, English, Farsi, French, German, Hebrew, Italian, Japanese, Korean, Portuguese, Russian, Spanish, and Tagalog.

♦ **Forex.com** (www.forex.com). You can open a mini account with US$250, but a standard account is US$2,500. Languages available include: Chinese, English, and Russian.

♦ **MG Financial Group** (www.mgforex.com). While you can open an account with a minimum of US$200, MG Financial Group recommends the minimum of US$1,000. Languages include Chinese, English, French, Russian, Spanish, and Urdu.

- ◆ **SNC Investments** (www.sncinvestment.com). You can open an account with a minimum of US$500. Languages available are English, French, Japanese, and Korean.

Note: The information listed for these Forex firms was taken from each company's website. This information can change, so please conduct thorough research prior to trading with any firm.

Appendix C

U.S. Regulatory Agencies

Forex can be a very risky way to trade. Luckily, some of that risk is minimized by the regulatory agencies involved in monitoring the world of Forex. Here are some of the top agencies that you should get to know.

Commodity Futures Trading Commission (www.cftc.gov)

The Commodity Futures Trading Commission (CFTC) has the jurisdiction and authority to investigate and take legal action to close down a wide assortment of unregulated firms offering or selling foreign currency futures and options contracts to the general public. In addition, the CFTC has jurisdiction to investigate and prosecute foreign currency fraud occurring in its registered firms and their affiliates. To find out more about its consumer-protection programs, go to www.cftc.gov/cftc/cftccustomer.htm.

You can write the CFTC at the following address:

Commodity Futures Trading Commission
Three LaFayette Centre
1155 21st Street, N.W.
Washington, DC 20581

You can ask a question, report information, or file a complaint by calling 866-366-2382.

The CFTC's e-mail address for complaints is enforcement@cftc.gov, or you can file a complaint online at www.cftc.gov/enf/enfform.htm.

National Futures Association

National Futures Association (NFA) is the regulatory organization for the U.S. futures industry, which also registers many of the brokers and dealers who serve Forex traders. Its mission is to safeguard market integrity, protect investors, and help its members meet their regulatory responsibilities.

Membership in NFA is mandatory for FCMs, but not for Forex dealers. They seek to ensure that everyone conducting business with the public on the U.S. futures exchanges—more than 4,200 firms and 55,000 associates—must adhere to the same high standards of professional conduct. NFA is an independent regulatory organization with no ties to any specific marketplace. It operates at no cost to the taxpayer. NFA is financed exclusively from membership dues and from assessment fees paid by the users of the futures markets.

The NFA maintains the Background Affiliation Status Information Center (BASIC), where you can find information about a Forex firm's CFTC registration and NFA membership information. You can also find regulatory and nonregulatory actions by the NFA and the CFTC. You can access BASIC online at www.nfa.futures.org/basicnet.

You can also file a complaint about a broker, dealer, or his firm at www.nfa.futures.org/basicnet/Complaint.aspx.

You can contact the NFA at one of its two offices:

Chicago Headquarters
200 W. Madison St., #1600
Chicago, IL 60606-3447
312-781-1300
312-781-1467 (fax)

New York Office
120 Broadway, #1125
New York, NY 10271
212-608-8660
212-964-3913 (fax)

Or you can call the NFA at 1-800-621-3570.

Other Regulatory Entities

The CFTC and NFA do regulate the majority of Forex firms, but it's possible that firms you are dealing with, or may deal with, are registered or regulated by other institutions or entities not under CFTC's jurisdiction. The following are the key regulatory entities that also may be able to help you if you are having a problem with a Forex trade involving one of their regulated entities.

Federal Deposit Insurance Corporation (www.fdic.gov)

If the bank you are dealing with is a chartered bank that is not a member of the Federal Reserve, then its chief regulator is the FDIC. This includes commercial and savings banks that are not in the Federal Reserve System. You can find resources for consumers at the FDIC website: www.fdic.gov/consumers/consumer/index.html. You can call the FDIC for information about a chartered bank at 877-275-3342. Or you can file a complaint or inquiry online at www2.fdic.gov/starsmail/index.asp.

If you want to reach the FDIC by mail, you need to write one of five office address in Washington, D.C. For a directory of key contacts in Washington, go to www.fdic.gov/about/contact/directory/index.html.

Federal Reserve Board (www.federalreserve.gov)

If you are dealing with a state-licensed bank that is a member of the Federal Reserve or a financial holding company, your best source for regulatory information is the Federal Reserve. You can research any enforcement actions against a bank at www.federalreserve.gov/boarddocs/enforcement.

You can contact the Federal Reserve Board of Governors as follows:

Board of Governors of the Federal Reserve System
20th Street and Constitution Avenue, NW
Washington, DC 20551
202-452-3000

Or you can find the nearest Federal Reserve Bank at the board's website at www.federalreserve.gov/FRAddress.htm.

National Credit Union Administration (www.ncua.gov)

The National Credit Union Administration is the regulatory agency you should contact if you are having a problem with a federal or state-chartered credit union. You can contact the Washington office as follows:

National Credit Union Administration
1775 Duke Street
Alexandria, VA 22314-3428
703-518-6300

The Office of the Comptroller of the Currency (www.occ.treas.gov)

The oldest of the financial regulators is the Office of the Comptroller of the Currency, which was founded in 1863 as a branch of the U.S. Department of Treasury. Today its role in the financial industry is to charter, regulate, and supervise all national banks, including their domestic and international activities.

If you have a complaint about a national bank, call the OCCC at its Consumer Assistance Group, 1-800-613-6743, or contact them by e-mail at customer.assistance@occ.tres.gov.

You can also contact the Consumer Assistance Group by mail:

Customer Assistance Group
1301 McKinney Street
Suite 3450
Houston, TX 77010

U.S. Securities and Exchange Commission (www.sec.gov)

If you are working with a firm that also trades securities, it is probably regulated by the U.S. Securities and Exchange Commission. You can file a complaint or send in a tip online at www.sec.gov/complaint.shtml.

You can call for consumer assistance on its information line at 1-800-732-0330.

You can contact the SEC's Washington headquarters as follows:

SEC Headquarters
100 F Street, NE
Washington, DC 20549
Office of Investor Education and Assistance
202-551-6551

Or you can e-mail them at help@sec.gov.

The SEC also has 12 regional offices. You can locate their contact information online at www.sec.gov/contact/addresses.htm.

State Regulators

You may also find additional information at your state attorney general's office and state banking, insurance, and securities regulators. You can find state websites on the Internet at www.statelocalgov.net.

CD Contents

The CD that comes with this book includes interactive links to key resources and currency information. It also includes a copy of the trading software DealBook® 360.

DealBook® 360 Software

If you no longer have the CD, you can download the current version of DealBook® 360 at www.gftforex.com/software/dealbookfx/download.asp.

In case you have lost the CD, the links are also listed below.

Key Resources

The following are a list of key regulatory agencies:

- ◆ Commodity Futures Trading Commission (www.cftc.gov)
- ◆ National Futures Association (www.nfa.futures.org)
- ◆ National Futures Association's Background Affiliation Status Information Center (www.nfa.futures.org/basicnet)
- ◆ North American Securities Administrators Association (www.nasaa.org/QuickLinks/ContactYourRegulator.cfm)

- National Association of Attorneys General (www.naag.org)
- Better Business Bureau (www.bbb.org)

The following are a list of key news sources about currency:

- Bloomberg (www.bloomberg.com)
- *Business Week* (www.businessweek.com)
- CNN Money (http://money.cnn.com)
- *Financial Times* (www.ft.com)
- *The Wall Street Journal* (www.wsj.com)

In addition to the major news media, several key Forex websites can help keep you informed about money trends:

- FX Street (www.fxstreet.com)
- Global Forex Trading (www.gftforex.com/resources)

The following are a list of exchanges for options on foreign currencies:

- Philadelphia Stock Exchange (www.phlx.com)
- Chicago Mercantile Exchange (www.cme.com)
- New York Board of Trade (www.nybot.com)

Interactive Currency Information

- U.S. State Department (www.state.gov/r/pa/ei/bgn/)

The following are a list of central banks:

- Reserve Bank of Australia (www.rba.gov.au)
- Bank of Canada (www.bankofcanada.ca/en/index.html)
- Czech National Bank (www.cnb.cz/en/index.html)
- Bank of England (www.bankofengland.co.uk)
- European Central Bank (www.ecb.int/home/html/index.en.html)

- Hong Kong Monetary Authority (www.info.gov.hk/hkma/eng/currency/link_ex/index.htm)

- Bank of Japan (www.boj.or.jp/en/)

- Reserve Bank of New Zealand (www.rbnz.govt.nz)

- South African Reserve Bank (www.resbank.co.za/navigate.htm)

- Swiss National Bank (www.snb.ch/e/index3.html)

- Central Bank of the Republic of Turkey (www.tcmb.gov.tr/yeni/eng/index.html)

- U.S. Federal Reserve (www.federalreserve.gov)

Other key web sources for the U.S. Federal Reserve include:

- New York Federal Reserve (www.newyorkfed.org/education/fx/foreign.html)

- The Fed's Beige Book (www.federalreserve.gov/FOMC/BeigeBook/2006/)

- The Fed's Fred (Federal Reserve Economic Data) (http://research.stlouisfed.org/fred2)

The following are a list of Forex settlement systems:

- BOJ-NET (www.boj.or.jp)

- CHAPS (www.bankofengland.co.uk/markets/paymentsystems)

- CHIPS (www.chips.org)

- CLS (www.cls-services.com/cls_bank)

- EURO 1 (www.abe.org)

- Fedwire (http://frbservices.org)

- PNS (www.banque-france.fr)

- POPS (www.bof.fi)

- TARGET (www.ecb.int/paym/target)

Index

T

technical analysis
  price patterns, 115
    channel, 115
    gaps, 116
    wedge, 115
  reading charts, 108-109
    bar charts, 110
    candlestick charts, 111
    line charts, 110
  spotting trends, 112
    drawing line, 112
    support and resistance,
      114-115
technical points, trade discipline,
  145
Thai baht (THB), 89
Thailand, emerging country
  currencies, 88-89
THB (Thai baht), 89
tick charts, 108
tight spreads, 153
Tilkin, Gary, 36-37
trade balances, fundamental
  analysis, 127-128
trade centers, 7
  brokers, 8-9
  commercial banks, 8
  corporations, 9
  dealers, 8-9
  governments, 8
  investment-management firms, 9
  speculators, 9-10
trade flows, fundamental analysis,
  122-123
traders, currency values, 55-56

trades
  discipline, 144-146
  keeping emotions in check,
    146-148
  percentage taking place, 5
placing orders
  broker/dealer selection,
    156-157
  GFT DealBook® 360,
    160-165
  leverage, 154-156
  profit/loss calculation,
    165-166
  terms, 151-154
  types, 157-160
platforms, 99-101
  computer hardware and
    software, 96-98
  Internet access, 98-99
  key information, 101-105
  retail platforms, 105-106
risk-management strategies,
  148
  limit orders, 148-149
  picking right points, 149-150
  stop-loss orders, 149
risks
  avoiding through regulated
    entities, 138
  counterparty, 133
  countries, 134-137
  exchange rate, 132
  interest rate, 132
  leverage, 130-131
  liquidity, 134
  market, 131
  volatility, 133-134

W-X-Y-Z

Check Out These
Best-Sellers